A
HOUSE
—·of·—
PRAYER

The POWER *of* PRAYING
IN COMMUNITY

THOMAS R. STEAGALD

UPPER
ROOM BOOKS®
NASHVILLE

Cover and interior design: Bruce DeRoos
Cover images: All images © Shutterstock.com

Library of Congress Cataloging-in-Publication Data

Steagald, Tom.
  A house of prayer : the power of praying in community / Thomas R. Steagald.
     pages cm
  ISBN 978-0-8358-1321-1 — ISBN 978-0-8358-1322-8 (mobi) — ISBN 978-0-8358-1323-5 (epub)
  1. Prayer—Christianity. 2. Public worship. I. Title.
  BV226.S74 2014
  248.3'2—dc23
                                    2013044548

Printed in the United States of America

DEDICATION

To Sadie Frances Nall Steagald
February 24, 1920–May 30, 2013

only daughter of Tom and Mattie,
only wife of Ray, only mother of Tom and Debs;
Grandmother and Great-Grandmother
Librarian, Sunday School Teacher, Caregiver

For thou, O Lord, art my hope,
my trust, O LORD, from my youth.
Upon thee I have leaned from my birth;
thou art he who took me from my mother's womb.
My praise is continually of thee.
PSALM 71:5-6 RSV

CONTENTS

PREFACE

Here the saying holds true, "One sows and another reaps." I sent you to reap that for which you did not labor. Others have labored, and you have entered into their labor.

JOHN 4:37-38

Not long ago, during a particularly stressful season of church ministry, my spiritual director (and friend) suggested I go into the sanctuary to pray, but "not those eloquent prayers you pray on Sunday mornings and at meetings. Simple prayers," she said. "Whatever your heart prompts you to say. *Raw.*"

I thought of the time Frederick Buechner's therapist told him to write with his left hand a dialogue between himself and his long-dead-by-suicide father. His right hand, a novelist's hand, formed words for effect, created and crafted meaning. Writing with his left hand might allow him to discover meanings deeper than he could invent.[1]

Wondering if I could pray "left-hearted," I entered the sanctuary and took a spot on the left side, the lectern side—away from the pulpit, away from "my" side. For what seemed the longest time I just sat there, restless and uncomfortable and alone. Voices behind me in the hallway signaled that Family Night supper was about to begin, but I did not want to see anyone. I hunkered down, hiding.

I tried to clear my mind. I tried to focus. I could do neither thing. I was jittery, as if the silence of the empty room were a predator closing in for the kill. I tried to turn off my brain and turn on my heart. Instead, my memory raced, careening through recent days and disappointments. I screwed my eyes shut against a fevered, erratic montage of hurtful images and painful discussions. All at once I felt caged, claustrophobic, panicked. I wanted to run away, but my legs would not work. I wanted to evaporate, to disappear. Never to be seen ever again.

"I don't *want* to be the pastor anymore," I growled to the pew in front of me. "Not here. Not *anywhere!*" I leaned back and saw the rafters of the sanctuary. They looked like the ribs of a ship, or a whale. I was Jonah, in the belly of the fish, squatting in salt water and darkness and vomit.

I do not know how long I sat there; less time than it felt like, I am sure. But snapping upright and snorting—enough of *this!*—I grabbed at the pew in front of me to wrench myself up in spite of my legs and get the hell out of there.

I was already standing, weakly, when I glanced down and saw *The United Methodist Hymnal* in the pew rack. My chin twitched. I paused. And then, as if my knees were water, I collapsed back into the seat. With trembling hand I reached for the hymnal and turned quickly to page 878, "An Order for Evening Praise and Prayer." How often had I turned to this very spot over the years? Prayed these very prayers? This time, though, when I looked down, it was as if I had never before seen them. These were not my prayers, but they were not *not* prayers, either.

Something urged, prodded me. *Just say it.* I took a breath, hesitated, looked around, and said it, but loudly enough for only myself to hear, "Light and peace in Jesus Christ."

I looked around again. I felt silly. "I could wish for light and peace," I muttered, shaking my head. I knew I was alone in the room, but I paused as if I were expecting someone to answer for once. And if I heard an answering word, would it be word enough to counter the loneliness of my prayer and ministry and life? To speak light into the darkness, peace into the turmoil? Who could say such a word? What might be said?

Could someone please say *something?* Anything? Anyone?

No one. Nothing.

But I plowed ahead: "Thanks be to God."

"Thanks for what?" I grumbled again, rolling my eyes at myself, unsure of why I was doing whatever I was doing. But in for a penny, in for a pound; almost defiantly I took another breath and shaped my mouth, said again the words that were at once so familiar to me and also so very strange: "We praise and thank you, O God. . . ."

And at the word *We* tears came, clawing their way out of my eyes as if seeking the light. My throat clutched. I looked down but could not see the words clearly. I knew them, though: "For you are without beginning and without end. Through Christ, you created the whole world; through Christ, you preserve it. You made the day for the works of light and the night for the refreshment of our minds and our bodies."

"*Our* minds and our bodies," I said again, as if I hadn't said this very phrase a thousand times before. It was like the first uncertain glimpse of land at dawn's horizon after the night's waves swamped the boat. I looked up from the foxhole to see that the promised rein-forcements had arrived. I had hit the mother lode with my last swing of the pick. I was on the verge of giving up, but with one word every-thing had changed, and me not least.

"Keep *us* now in Christ," I said, my heart swelling, my voice ris-ing. "Grant *us* a peaceful evening, a night free from sin; and bring *us* at last to eternal life [*us, Us, US!*]. . . . Through Christ our Lord. . . . Amen."

Our Lord! Amen and amen!

Tears flowed and I knew, I *knew*, that I was not alone. Not at all. I was not even *praying* alone. No matter what I felt or didn't feel when I began the liturgy, the liturgy itself proved that I was praying with others, even in that moment. I was part of the community, the family of God, the body of Christ. I may have been by myself in the sanctuary, but I was one of many—only one, yes, but *one* of the great *we* that is the church.

Somewhere other believers were also praying these same words— or words very similar to them. Parishioners who had prayed with me in the past were praying with me too, if only in my memory.

Saints and apostles, prophets and martyrs—the whole company of heaven on that distant shore in a greater light (but near as my heart and breath and darkness)—they too were praying with and for me. And Jesus, not least! Jesus too was praying for me and with me, as he prays *for* and *with* and *in* all of us (Rom. 8:34); as we indeed pray with and in him.

I was not praying alone. I was not even praying my own prayer! I was praying a given prayer: prayer given as a gift of light, of harbor; of reinforcement and treasure.

It was a most powerful moment for me. And though this book was already well on its way to completion, my time in the sanctuary that evening crystallized for me the premise and the promise of communal prayer, and also its joy and power: that at all times and in all places we are part of a family, a praying body, even in those moments and seasons when it seems or feels as if we pray in isolation.

We are part of a tradition, that is to say, part of a people, a history, a Way of living and thinking and praying *otherwise*. Consequently, anytime we pray *our* prayers, we are praying together (even when we are "praying together, apart,"[2] as Lauren Winner describes it). If we listen, by grace we will hear other voices under and above and alongside our own, voices before us and behind us. And we will discover, or remember, that we are deeply, intimately, even eternally connected. We do not pray or think or live alone. That is part of what it means to say we believe "in the communion of the saints."

Sometimes we are blessed to pray together *physically*: to share the same air, to say the same exact words at the same exact moment; to stand shoulder to shoulder and heart to heart. In such moments the saintly communion is made *manifest*, and we find ourselves both formed and transformed. In praying together we *become* once and again (and more each time) the body of Christ, the once and current and future family of God.

God is ever at work gathering his children to himself and one another, despite lines and walls and even enmities. Across time and space too. By means of the liturgy, the Hours, the traditions of our faith, God grants us to pray together with our elders and children, with our near neighbors and those who are on the other side of the world or circumstance. Our communal praying forms and transforms us into a "chosen race, a royal priesthood, a holy nation, God's own people" (1 Peter 2:9). So formed and increasingly transformed, we "set our faces" against the militant and atomizing fragmentation of the prevailing culture.

"Closing ranks" with one another, though, does not insulate or isolate us. Quite the contrary. Our prayers throw open the doors, invite others in while we prepare the Bath and set the Table for any lonely pilgrim who would dwell with us in the house of the Lord forever.

In sum, when despite all our differences and disagreements we pray our prayers together, the future of the world appears and is made evident. In that way our prayers are deeply sacramental, the very means of God's uniting and unifying grace. The prayers convey what they signify, that we are and will be one, even as Jesus prayed that we would be.

———— • ————

I want to thank the ones who, sometimes in proximity and sometimes apart, have prayed together both for me and with me as I sketched, framed, and finished this little "room," this little monastic cell of a book, where for a couple of years now I have retreated, struggled, pondered, and offered to God my best insights and stories. I now offer them to you, with gratitude to Jeannie, my editor at Upper Room Books, who embraced the idea so enthusiastically; also to Liz, another editor, who, though she was not involved with this particular volume, edited other books of mine and lovingly chiseled me into more of a writer than I could have been without her gracious hammerings.

I want to thank Mike, Bruce, Doris, and Lyn, who read all or parts of this material before it was published. Thanks also to Debra at *The Christian Century*; and to David and all the "goodpeople" at www.goodpreacher.com (including, now, those at Luther Seminary), who have kept me blogging, thereby giving me time and reason for reflection. Thanks as well to the Lilly Endowment Inc., the

Collegeville Institute at Saint John's University, and Mary Nilsen and my colleagues there during a writing week in the summer of 2012.

I also want to thank the people of Lafayette Street United Methodist Church for their love and support through a dark and difficult season in my life and ministry. They helped me develop many of these ideas without even knowing they did so.

A father's love, as always, to Bethany, and her husband, Rob; to Jacob, and whoever his girlfriend might be when this book is published. Love to my sister, Debs, too and her husband, Chuck.

A special word of thanks to Ruth and Paul, to David and Lissa, for their generous hospitality: they gave me beautiful sanctuary at their homes-away-from home, and uninterrupted time to write.

An odd thanks, this: to Dr. Jonathan Haidt, a professor at the University of Virginia, whom I have never met but whose book *The Righteous Mind: Why Good People Are Divided by Politics and Religion* spurred my thinking and is a constant (if not always overt) conversation partner with me in these pages. Dr. Haidt's is the one book I unfailingly recommend to my students and friends.

This book is dedicated to my mother, who died while I was finishing the manuscript but just before then helped me travel to the Holy Land (you will come to see why that is important for these reflections). More importantly and long ago, she gave me the best book I ever received: *A Diary of Private Prayer*, by John Baillie. On the one hand, "private prayer" seems out of keeping with the thesis of the book I am writing. But, as I will suggest and have already narrated, the personal and the communal are not at all contradictory. Should we pray only one way or the other, we rob prayer of its full effect.

Even more to the point, with publication Dr. Baillie's prayers ceased being private at all, and it was as I prayed his prayers, earnestly, daily, for long months (and not least the prayer at the head of this preface) that I began to realize the pastoral, prophetic, and even evangelistic power of Christian people's praying together.

THOMAS R. STEAGALD
Lent, 2013

INTRODUCTION

———————◆———————

If somebody comes to me and says, "Teach me how to pray," I say, "Be at this church at nine o'clock on Sunday morning." That's where you learn how to pray. Of course, prayer is continued and has alternate forms when you're by yourself. But the American experience [of prayer] has the order reversed. In the long history of Christian spirituality, community prayer is most important, then individual prayer.

EUGENE PETERSON

Frederick Buechner has written that everyone prays, whether they know it or not. He has in mind the "Help me, pleases!" and "Thank yous!" that are voiced to Whoever may be listening at a moment of perceived rescue or bounty, and also the silent nods of reverence or slack-jawed wonderments at creation's wild beauty. Everyone who breathes prays sometime, he writes, in some way.[1] It has always and everywhere been so.

That is a good thing, of course, and we might leave it at that and be on our pilgrim way, thanking God for the uniform experience of spontaneous prayer. But we might also note that such prayers are mostly situational and solitary offerings, with scant relational aspect. These prayers have even less power to form or transform, to change lives or build communities. They are prayers prayed alone.

But formation, which is to say the making and shaping of faithful community, has been the very nerve and goal of prayer since well before the psalmist set pen to parchment. Doxology and thanks, confession and intercession—even petition, if it is done rightly—are constitutive. This syllabus of praying gradually transforms individuals into members of the family of God, the body of Christ. If, though, the primary posture of prayer in our culture is "alone" and if the forms and context of prayers are ignored—in short, if our primary understanding and experience of prayer is backward—then we already have a nascent insight into why so many people are dissatisfied with their prayer lives. Why do so many praying Christians feel as if their prayers "die at the ceiling" or echo in the dark? Perhaps something crucial is *missing*.

I suggest that what's missing is the sense and the experience of deep connection and real community: of spiritual intimacy not only with God but with other praying believers. Believing and praying others, members of our spiritual family who gather with us around Word, Table, Bath, and Hours, are a gift of God to absorb the echo of isolated orisons. Believing, praying others help us hoist before God the concerns that are too heavy for any one of us alone to lift "past the ceiling."

I believe God has placed it in our hearts to pray *together*: to meet in some place and time, to give ourselves to some form or fashion, to pray both with and for one another. When we don't pray like that, or do so only rarely, we sense the loss even if we cannot articulate it—as when we hunger for something we cannot name.

Praying in unison or even responsively is a feature of most liturgical worship, of course. Many worshipers are accustomed to praying a collect or joining in a litany of confession or thanksgiving. There is the Great Thanksgiving too, a part of Holy Communion, though many worshipers may be surprised to discover that the Great Thanksgiving is in fact a *prayer*. But these occasional, formal prayers may be the exception to prove the "rule" of American spirituality as Peterson described it and *so* occasional and exceptional as to invalidate the exercise. That is, for many American worshipers, even in traditionally sacramental or liturgical churches, collects or litanies may not *feel* like real *praying* at all—or even "qualify" as *real* prayer.

How did we find ourselves in this predicament? Which is to say, why is corporate prayer in eclipse?

I think the reasons are both cultural/psychological and religious/spiritual, with roots in the American dream and American revivalism.

Revivalism and Prayer

American religious sensibilities are yet beholden to the great "revivals" of our American religious heritage. The First, Second, and Third Great Awakenings swept across our land beginning in the eighteenth century and lasted until the early twentieth century.[2] One component of the revivals' message was a call for those who desired "religious *experience*" to repudiate all "outward forms," whether liturgy, rituals, prayer books—even "religion" itself—*things* that, while purporting to mediate God's presence, actually impeded God's work.[3] To be desired was the immediacy of God's presence, the unhindered power of the Holy Spirit, the inward witness, and a "personal relationship" with Jesus.

For many, the *community* of faith, the church and its traditions, was itself a hindrance to spiritual vitality. Christian life was conceived, received, and expressed in increasingly individualistic terms. With time, "personal" became private, the private became subjective, and the subjective became relative.[4] There was no authority outside the self, no accountability beyond "me and Jesus," and no "truth" other than "my truth." Preaching existed primarily to help an individual obtain God's promises now and later.

Fast forward. No wonder that even now, in times of economic hardship, the preachers of prosperity theology (modern incarnations of the great revivalists such as Charles Finney[5]) have, well, prospered. These television icons have found a way to proclaim the culture's dominant materialism in the language of individual spirituality, sprinkled with a pixie-dust residue of Manifest Destiny: "This is what God wills for you."[6]

But the least deconstruction of this kind of preaching reveals the underpinnings of prosperity theology (and so many other less ostentatious examples of what Michael Horton calls the "alternative gospel of the American church"[7]) to be, not so much covenantal and providential, but Gnostic and Pelagian: a given preacher has "special knowledge" ("These seven steps deliver your best life now!"); and "if you do your part," you will be prosperous because God helps those who help themselves! In sum, these preachers have found a way to align the last remaining vestiges of our revivalistic roots with the American dream.[8]

This understanding of the Christian faith and life offers no resource beyond the self, no comfort beyond the circumstantial, no compelling sense of power to either form us or transform us, and neither summons nor strategy for serving or changing the world. A "faith" construed in such terms may be true to the culture but not to the gospel.

WEIRD Prayers

Worship is a pitched battle in what may be called an epic "culture war." I am not, by that term, referring to the partisan and politicized debate joined across a range of hot-button social issues. I am speaking, rather, of the deeper and more essential conflict between the "church militant," with its communal summons and commission, and the hyperindividualized society, with its "gospel" of self.

In *The Righteous Mind: Why Good People Are Divided by Politics and Religion*,[9] University of Virginia psychologist Jonathan Haidt characterizes our culture as WEIRD, an acronym coined by Joe Henrich, Steve Heine, and Ara Norenzayan in 2010. WEIRD stands for: "Western, educated, industrialized, rich, and democratic."[10] Dr. Haidt writes that "several of the peculiarities of WEIRD culture can be captured in this simple generalization: *The WEIRDer you are, the more you see a world full of separate objects, rather than relationships.*"[11] The illustration he uses is powerful:

> *When asked to write twenty statements beginning with the words "I am . . . ," Americans are likely to list their own internal psychological characteristics (happy, outgoing, interested in jazz), whereas East Asians are more likely to list their roles*

*and relationships (a son, a husband, an employee of Fujitsu).
. . . Putting this all together, it makes sense that WEIRD phi-
losophers since Kant and Mill have mostly generated moral
systems that are individualistic, rule-based, and universalist.
That's the morality you need to govern a society of autonomous
individuals.*[12]

Dr. Haidt writes that "the moral domain is unusually narrow in WEIRD cultures, where it is largely limited to the ethic of
autonomy."[13] That autonomous lens, worn long enough, produces
spiritual myopia: makes it hard to see or understand the value of
other ways of seeing and living—the communal and relational, for
instance; the deferential or sacred.

If Dr. Haidt is right, then in this time and culture even Christian
people come to worship seeing themselves as more or less autonomous (with families, perhaps, or associations, but that barely widens
the perspective). They see other worshipers too as discrete and separate selves, and maybe even the church itself as but a loosely associated group of individuals. Moreover, along with the rest of their
cultural peers, these individuals have been taught to make judgments
based on personal opinion, preference, and even prejudice. Consequently, the predicate of the worship experience, and its most compelling interpretive grid is *self: my* tastes and preferences, whether in
music or worship style or leadership.

But, in fact, the moral domain of the church and its worship,
rooted as it is in Word and sacrament as well as in the characteristic
summons of the gospel itself, is hardly concerned with autonomy
at all. The call is to community; the commission is cosmic. And so
believers are left with the deep—if often unrecognized, unacknowl-
edged, and unarticulated—dissonance between the *ethos* of the
church and its gospel, and the cultural predispositions of most Sunday morning worshipers.

To use the language of Ephesians 6:12, the church and its gospel
are contending not against flesh and blood but against the powerful principles of this age. The sharp contrast between the relational
message of the gospel, its worship and peacemaking mission, and

the WEIRD individualistic way we are accustomed to interpreting our lives and world may also give us some understanding as to why the church in America is declining. If what we might call "the communal nature of the gospel" makes less and less compelling sense in a hyperindividualistic culture, in those places and among those people where ever-wider associations are valued, there is good and fertile ground to receive gospel seed.

Private and Public Prayers

John Wesley, in his "Third General Rule," called on early Methodists to offer both private and public prayers.[14] Wesley knew that there are times to pray alone, to pray in the privacy of one's heart and soul, and to pray with one's family as well.

But Wesley also knew of and believed in the power and necessity of praying with one's spiritual family, with brothers and sisters in the faith. His classes and societies proved that when Christians pray together or begin to pray together or begin to learn to pray together, they may also begin to discover and enjoy—and benefit—from prayer's full effect. Prayer has *pastoral* power to transform us and our communities, *prophetic* power to help us be in the world but not of it, to stand together in but against our fractured and fragmenting culture, and *evangelistic* power to welcome weary pilgrims home. Praying for and with our brothers and sisters *effects*—helps to form and forge—the very fellowship and community that are at the heart of what it means to *be* the church. Which is to say, praying together empowers us.

Jesus said, "My house shall be called a house of prayer" (Matt. 21:13, quoting Isa. 56:7). Consider this book an invitation to enter, either again or for the first time, the house of prayer. But I am inviting you to discover and enjoy the great gifts we have been given: repositories of prayers; patterns of praying; a way to *be* the family of God with and for one another. This form of praying and these prayers, far from hindering personal experience, deepen our intimacy with God and with our spiritual friends, forming and nurturing real

Christian community. Such prayers and praying are exercises in tradition, faith, and hope.

As to *tradition*, with its other gifts, communal praying offers contemporary place and voice to our elders in the faith—and joins us to our heritage. Such praying is no exercise in nostalgia, however—our minds and voices returning to a dead past. Rather, the form and substance of communal prayer let us stand with those who lived their lives and died their deaths for our sake. By their faith and example we have source and resource for our own generation's journey, even as we receive and enjoy the benefits of their wisdom, hope, and joy.

Communal praying is an act of *faith*, a means by which we form deep and lasting commitment and community in the present. Across geography and class, language and practice, politics and persuasion, gender and orientation, and the vast host of lesser walls that divide us, praying together forms us into *a faithful people*. We are granted a foretaste of the very future of God's purposes for the world.

Accordingly, praying together reorients us toward that future. As such it is an exercise in *hope*. Jesus prayed, "Holy Father, keep them in thy name . . . that they may be one, even as we are one" (John 17:11, RSV). We believe Jesus continues to pray that prayer (Rom. 8:34); and when we pray *as one* we both answer his prayer and join our lives to his hope.

Praying together, then, becomes an invitation and, indeed, a motivation for "all who . . . seek to live in peace with one another" to turn away from the isolations and enmities fostered by our culture and toward the divinely ordained future. Our prayers enable us in a very basic and practical way to embrace and incarnate—and to help build—the kingdom of God.

This book encourages its readers to enter the house of prayer, and to examine their own praying in light of the community that Christ has ordained across space and time. The hope is that as *we* redirect and refocus our prayers—and as our prayers refocus and redirect us—as together *we* pray to God with all of our hearts, souls, minds, and strength, and for neighbor and others as much or more than ourselves, our prayers will be an exercise in love. They will help us obey Jesus' command to love God completely and everyone else as he loved us.

If we can do that, we may find that our churches will once again become, as Jesus described them, houses of prayer. And vibrant. We will still go into our rooms, pray in the privacy of our own hearts and minds and experiences. But that is not the only place we will pray—or even the primary place. And we will begin to or again feel ourselves connected both to God and to one another.

We will more nearly be the church into which Jesus called us each and all.

1

THE PREMISE OF PRAYER

Ignorance and sin are characteristic of isolated individuals.
Only in the unity of the Church do we find these defects overcome.
Man [sic] finds his true self in the Church alone; not in the helplessness
of spiritual isolation but in the strength of his communion
with his brothers [and sisters] and his Saviour.

ALEXANDER ELCHANINOV

N ot long ago, with another fifty pilgrims or so, my son and I
visited the Holy Land. We spent the first part of our trip in the
Galilee, in the north of Israel, where the landscape is relatively lush
and green. On our first full day there we went to Yardenit, the "traditional site" of Jesus' baptism, dressed-up and commercialized, the
place where television evangelists take groups for photos and reim-
mersions; where "the Wall of New Life" renders on tile the story of
Jesus' baptism in fifty or more languages. But Yardenit is not the place.

John the Baptist preached in the wilderness, and there is no wilderness in the Galilee. Officials designated Yardenit as Jesus' baptismal spot mostly for the sake of tourism so pilgrims would have a safe
place on the Jordan River to visit and remember. And also because
another site, farther south—a spot rather recently and rather reliably
suggested as a possible place of Jesus' baptism—was for long years

inaccessible on account of residual, simmering hostilities after the Six-Day War.

Some groups go there now, though, and ours was one of them.

The morning of our third day in Israel, we boarded our bus and headed south. We left the Galilee and its greenhoused agricultural magnificence. After a while we were surrounded by wilderness—flat dusty desert with gray boulders and steep, sharp outcroppings. The Jordan, muddy and sweet, in some places a trickle and in others a white-water surge, more or less bisects this barren terrain, and our driver more or less followed the river.

The farther south we went, the less natural vegetation we saw, save on the banks of the holy river. On either side of the Jordan we could see great trees, their ancient roots dug deep into the dry desert to siphon life from that ancient aquifer. The sight gave me, and our entire entourage, a whole new appreciation for Psalm 1:1-3:

Happy are those . . .
[whose] delight is in the law of the LORD,
and on his law they meditate day and night.
They are like trees
planted by streams of water,
which yield their fruit in its season,
and their leaves do not wither.
In all that they do, they prosper.

John preached and baptized in a place somewhere near this very place, east and a bit north of Jerusalem, where the topography itself bears witness to stark alternatives: wilderness and death; water and life. Jesus came into this very wilderness, to this very river, to be baptized by John. No one can know for sure, of course, exactly where in that holy water John and Jesus met that day, but we were getting close to the place or what might have been the place or what the actual place more or less looked like.

A couple of hours after we boarded the bus, we turned east off the highway and onto a longish dirt-and-gravel road flanked by bombed-out bunkers, pockmarked concrete, and, all along the way, barbed-wire fences. Bright yellow signs, too many of them, with arresting red lettering, urgently festooned the fencing.

We could see churches even before we got off the bus: tall gold domes of the Russian Orthodox above the tree line, flashing, reflecting all but blinding light even on a sunny day; multiple crosses and tall steeples on both sides of the river's banks; churches under construction and at least one church, Greek Orthodox, that was not only unfinished but apparently abandoned, though a Greek flag still flapped in the breeze.

There were a few other buses too. In the parking lot and gift shop we saw tourist-pilgrims not a few—though not nearly as many as we had seen in Yardenit, where the bright tiles and immense retail area put me in mind of Disney World.

We started toward the river, toward the bank of *our* side, one could say. We passed two young Israeli soldiers with AK-47s slung over their shoulders. They smiled small, taut smiles, nodding their yarmulked heads only slightly when we waved and grinned.

Wooden steps took us to the water, which in that spot is maybe one hundred feet wide or less: about as wide as a sanctuary. Our guide said, "The river is the border between Israel and, on the other side, the nation of Jordan."

As if cued, we looked across to the Jordanian side and saw a lone Jordanian soldier, older than his Israeli counterparts but with an AK-47 on *his* shoulder. Soon, wars may be fought over water more than oil, and soldiers on both sides are already armed for it. The land too is armed: those yellow signs with the red lettering warned us of land mines.

There were land mines everywhere, even right up behind the gift shop. We were warned and warned again to stay on this side of the barbed wire, but I don't think anyone was of a mind to wander.

At the water's edge our group sang and prayed. Other groups alongside us did the same. We captured some of that holy, muddy water in Dixie cups and renewed our baptisms, the preachers among us pressing the Jordan like a cross onto the foreheads of the others and then onto one another's too. "Remember your baptism and be thankful," we said over and over. "Amen," we all said in turn.

My son and I went down into the river to pray. Standing calf-deep, arm in arm in that holy flow, we noticed that on the *other* side, the Jordanian side, other pilgrims, Arab Christians, were coming to the water just as we had. They passed the soldier and his gun, descended the steps, touched and stood in the Jordan, were baptized in the Jordan or renewed their baptisms—that moment and that river just as holy to them on their side of the political divide as it was to us on our side of it.

And it suddenly occurred to me that for all the sharp divisions that wet place in the dry wilderness represents—all the warring politics, all the fear, all the thin-lipped and weaponized tensions that turn young men into old men before their time—that holy water is not just, or even mostly, a *dividing* place. It is, rather, a uniting place: where fathers and sons, mothers and daughters, Jordanians and Israelis, Americans and Russians, Jews and Greeks and Arabs, and just about everyone else you can name, are invited to come as they are, to honor a glorious past and to embrace an as-yet-unrealized future. Even now, we can go down into the water to pray, all of us equal in the eyes of God, offering up prayers for the aquifer of peace.

There is deep hunger in us for peace, a deep thirst for what water is and means. All of us need and desire a holy bathing and in that same holy water, to be washed clean of the world and its warring madness, the easy enmities of the prevailing culture.

And if we can name that hunger, see that need, then maybe we can begin to see that we need one another too, just as we are. Alone, divided, we cannot do what Jesus commanded. More fundamentally even than that, Jesus died to break down the walls between us, to free us from separations and divisions. Which is to say, if there is to be peace on earth and if it is to begin with us, it will begin when we all come again to the waters of our baptisms—whether in Israel or in our sanctuaries or in our memories—when we remember our baptisms and are truly thankful and when we pray together for one another in the damp holiness of such celebration and remembrance.

A House (of Prayer) Divided

I grew up in the Bible Belt—in its very buckle! The flames of the revivals were still burning in those days. They smolder even now in some places. And sometimes, I confess, I still feel the heat and warm myself by the fires of memory.

I heard many a sermon on prayer, but the basic thrust was always this: prayer is what you do, as the old Bible says, when you "go into your closet." You go into your closet or room and shut the door, and there, alone, you pray to your Father in secret. . . . The takeaway was clear: true believers do not practice their piety before others; they do not heap up empty phrases; they do not emulate the hypocrites, the formally "religious" who love to be *seen* praying. They certainly do not pray the prayers of others or make use of written prayers. A written prayer was no prayer.

The preachers invariably cited Matthew 6:6, where even in the Greek original[1] Jesus said that prayer, along with the giving of alms (6:2), is a private matter between the believer and God alone. Praying and giving—both offerings (one to God, one to neighbor)—were to be done without notice and without desire for notice: in *secret*, just as Jesus said.

Initially planted by the preachers of the Great Awakenings, this camp meeting "seed" of personal/private religious experience was further cultivated in the revivals of my youth. And though we are long since removed chronologically from the historic revivals, even now this primarily personal/private view of spirituality and prayer is for many Christians their "default" setting—and deeply rooted in the many and various forms of mainstream American spiritual consciousness.[2]

For a truth, Jesus did say what he said in Matthew 6:6. The revivalists were partly right, quite appropriately critiquing any "form of godliness" that denied its power (2 Tim. 3:5). John Wesley offered a similar jeremiad against the Anglicanism of his own day.

But Jesus said more and other than *only* that, and his instructions related to prayer are not limited to that one verse in the Sermon on the Mount. In the other prayer and piety passages[3]—and even in that one chapter!—Jesus gives instructions to the disciples *together*.

Recall how the Sermon on the Mount begins: Jesus sees the crowds, goes up the mountain, *sits down* (Matt. 5:1-2). Sitting is the traditional posture for a rabbi when he teaches. When Jesus' disciples came to him, Jesus "opened his mouth and taught them, saying. . . ." Jesus continues teaching *them* throughout the sermon, of course; and even in chapter 6, with the exception of verse 6, when Jesus teaches on prayer and piety, all the Greek pronouns and verbs are *plural*.

We easily miss that fact and its significance, for in standard English there is no adequate second person plural. We most often hear "you" as second person singular. But if we were to translate Matthew's Greek into *Southern* English, as it were, what we would hear is that Jesus is not saying "you" much at all but "*y'all*."

Time and again, Jesus says, "When *y'all* pray . . ."

"When y'all pray, pray like this: '*Our* Father . . .'"

In sum, the revivalists were partly right. Jesus believed in, practiced, even instructed his disciples in the discipline of private prayer: prayer in the first person singular. But all the more, Jesus believed in, practiced, and instructed his disciples in the disciplines and duty of praying in the first person plural. Jesus does not, in other words, advocate private prayer at the expense of corporate prayer. Quite the contrary! As a Jewish rabbi, steeped in the traditions of his heritage and faith community, Jesus preached and practiced the power of faithful community. From the very first he called his disciples into fellowship and partnership.

That same call continues even now—though praying together is not something we have been taught to do, or at least, not encouraged to do save for occasional moments during Sunday morning worship. Jesus' message, even for us, seems to be that the foundation and *context* for private prayer is the community and *its* prayers. Corporate prayer is to be supplemented and supported by private prayer, but praying together is crucial.

Naming the Dragon's Heads

A question.

If you were going to choose an adjective to describe the current ethos of our age and context, might *individualistic* be among your first choices?

The word *individualistic* is more or less value-neutral. It is a good thing, psychologically, to be individuated, your own unique person. It is a good thing, spiritually, to be all God intended *you* to be in the particularity of your aptitudes, environment, and circumstances. It is a good and godly thing, ecclesiastically, to be one among the many, a member of the body of Christ, to employ the gifts and graces God has given you for the benefit of the church, and to receive from others the gifts God has given them. These good things may be unrealized or, worse, lost in dark shadows when individuation produces isolation, or when self-development becomes self-absorption.

When self-awareness tends to narcissism, or egocentricity births anger and loneliness—in short, when individuality is set over against the community, and each of us is so determined to be his or her "own person" that we are left without a people—then a good thing becomes a very bad thing indeed.

Without *others*, without a compelling sense of *community*, more and deeper than occasional or superficial connection, we are atomized—"islandated," as one of my friends describes it. Such a narrowed identity is not only unsatisfying but also unsustainable. Such existence is not life as God intended it. Such a "faith" is sundered from its ethical moorings.

In this isolated land of dark shadows, prayer too is diminished. Designed to form and conform and transform us by praise, thanks, and intercession and (when our contrition is perfect; see chapter 6) confession, our prayers and we ourselves instead are stunted, withered, choked off as if by the weeds of pure petition—self-centered desires expressed most often in strings of self-serving requests.

The point is this: a good thing, that we each are created in God's image, can be corrupted when the point of emphasis is solely on the "each," and when others become "other." But when we remember that God has created us each *for* each other and that Jesus called us *into* community, when we remember that Jesus lived and died to break down dividing walls to make the many "one" and that the Holy Spirit and the holy church would engage us in those spiritual practices (worship, the sacraments, prayer) that forge, form, and strengthen community, we are on our way back to the light.

From the start God determined that it was not good for us to be alone. The first chapters of Genesis show us that only together are we, in fact, made in the full image of God. God called to Abram in order to make of him a *people*, a nation. God's covenant was with Israel as a whole. Jesus called disciples, made a church, a family, out of people who would not have gone to dinner together on a bet—a Zealot *and* a publican? At the same table? Who could have imagined it?

Paul talked of the body of Christ and each of us members of it: mutually dependent and also mutually obligated; mutually submissive too: not insisting on our own way but regarding others as better than ourselves, doing nothing from selfish ambition and conceit, experiencing and sharing a ministry and message of reconciliation. Call it the gospel's *ethos*.

But our culture does not interpret or encourage life in these terms. Accordingly, when I contend that the church is engaged in a "culture war," I am not referencing the partisan wranglings across a spectrum of social issues usually implied by the term. No, I am speaking of a much broader war than that; a much deeper conflict, a more essential and consequential struggle.

In Revelation 12, John tells us of a woman clothed with the sun and the moon under her feet and on her head a crown of twelve stars—and is it Mary? Some say so, because the woman is pregnant, crying out in the anguish of childbirth. More likely John means the church itself—right then, "another portent appeared in heaven: behold, a great red dragon, with seven heads and ten horns, and seven diadems upon his heads. His tail swept down a third of the stars of heaven, and cast them to the earth" (12:3-4, RSV).

The red dragon faced the crying woman, stood before her so as to devour her male child—and no doubt this time who it is: it is Jesus, who will rule the nations with a rod of iron, John said—but the child was caught up to God, and the woman fled to the wilderness, and war broke out between Michael and his angels, and the dragon and his angels.

The ancient enemy and the ongoing battle: this is the stuff of hymns and apocalypses. And, as John laments, the great red dragon makes some headway: his tail sweeps down a third of the stars in heaven. Still, only a third. A third of the saints are lost, but the war will be won. In the end.

But until then the battle continues, a sometimes violent grappling between the forces of light and the forces of darkness, between righteousness and evil, between the dragon and the church—and we can find ourselves caught up into it. Still, the struggle is not always so obvious as John's image, the "dragon" not always so visible. The battle is not always even "outside," in the heavens or on the earth.

What John seems to have in mind when he sees the dragon is Rome: the city built on seven hills, with ten great emperors: Rome occupied Jerusalem and persecuted the people of God. Romans beat, whipped, and crucified Jesus, tried to devour him and his followers but could not. Roman authorities persecuted, tortured, killed some of Jesus' disciples. But Rome itself fell; the dragon was destroyed. That is the story John tells in Revelation: not the end of the world but the end of Rome.

But whatever the "discreet history" or meaning of a biblical text, many other meanings are present. John may have Rome in mind, but he both describes and condemns all empires, and not only ancient ones, that by their arrogance and weaponry enforce their own version of peace over against the vision of God's kingdom. John describes and condemns all lesser rulers and authorities too, and cultural as much as political, along with all lesser powers and principalities, and not least the kind of psychological myopathies that blind us to the will and work of God.

I have been thinking about that red dragon, that seven-headed monster that rises up to wage war on the church, its worship and mission. And how, in our day, might the dragon stand before us to devour our witness and faithfulness? Perhaps by atomizing us? By sweeping us down "from the heavens" to the earth, to the realm of merely earthly concerns?

Surely I am not the first to compare the seven heads of the dragon with the seven deadly sins! I may be the first to compare our cultural ethos with the dragon itself, standing ever before us and ready to devour every birthing of faith and faithfulness by means of anger, pride, lust, greed, envy, despair, or sloth—each of them terribly isolating temptations with community-destroying power.

Each head's razor-sharp teeth deliver toxic venom, leave terrible and slow-to-heal scars in individuals' hearts and lives, and thereby in congregations and traditions.

Anger: Not the good kind of momentary anger that flashes and inspires us to protect our children or right a societal wrong, but the kind of anger that we feed and stoke, that smolders and pollutes, grudge-holding, easy-offense-taking anger that drives a wedge between us and our brothers and sisters, that creates space, when Jesus died to bring us together.

Pride: Not self-respect or divinely given confidence, and always attended by humility; but self-importance, self-absorption, self-obsession, self-aggrandizement that ultimately produces embittered isolation.

Lust: Not just inappropriate sexual desire, but *objectification*, the flattening, the self-gratifying and self-satisfying *use* (whether by ravenous regard or callous disregard) of people and things.

Greed: Whatever I/we have is not enough.

Envy: Whatever they have is what I/we have to have. The standard is they, whoever "they" are; or some assumed "bar," whatever it is, and the only consequence is dissatisfaction and anger.

Despair: The past is only regret, the future is only dread, and the present is only misery. Even God cannot make it better. There is no light, no hope, no peace, nor shall there ever be.

Sloth: Not simply laziness but serial distraction, unfocused but busy boredom: no time to see the burning bush, even if one appears, and no time to answer God's call because you have to take this *other* call, answer this e-mail, or grab some lunch before the next activity or appointment.

Sometimes the battle we wage is outside ourselves, fierce and loud, and we can count the casualties: prophets, workers, people.

Sometimes we see the dragon, red and fierce! But more often, far more often, we wage the battle in our heart and mind, in our prayers and worship, when the cultural dragon devours the gospel of peace and reconciliation. Sadly, we go to lunch unaware when we have been bitten: cannot always feel it when our souls are wounded or know when we have been swept down to the realm of the banal.

John vividly reminds us that the battle continues and will till the end. For now, no less than at any other time we know, the church remains in the wilderness, exiled by the threat of the dragon. (Even our own personal seven-headed monsters will not be defeated finally till our last breath, till we drag the beast through the Jordan: only those holy waters can finally slay red dragons.)

Till then, we remain officially at war against the beast—and in our case against this narcissistic culture whose idiom even we who claim the cross know so well. The dragon is *always* present—sometimes "out there" but always "in here," in each heart and every congregation, those seven heads snapping at us, dividing us, wanting to devour our commitment, to swallow up mission, to sweep us down.

Back to Basics

The premise of prayer is the premise of the gospel, the culmination of God's purpose for the world: The end of enmity and the re-creation of the world: sabbath. That is the beginning and the conclusion of the biblical narrative and the hope of all God's children. We read the Bible to remind ourselves of our place in the Story and our purpose.

For those who get lost in the Bible, however, and roughly following N. T. Wright's account,[4] I offer this summary as a way of helping us find our spiritual bearings:

1. God created the world, everything in and around it, and behold, it was *very* good.
2. But something went way out of whack, awful bad wrong, so that the world and its people languished under the weight of their disobedience and indifference.
3. God chose Abraham and his heirs, sent the Law, the prophets, the priests, and the kings as instruments of God's healing and

peace—but to no lasting avail.

4. In the fullness of time, God sent Jesus—the Word became Jewish flesh to heal the whole world, to save God's children in a way the Law, the prophets, and the Temple could not.

5. Jesus called disciples, then and now, to be his students, the flesh of his word, the body of Christ, to continue that healing and saving work.

In that story, in our sacraments and our scriptures, we proclaim and discover again who we are, where we are, our real purpose: God was in Christ and Christ is in us; God sent Jesus and Jesus sends us.

The Word became flesh, so that our flesh might become God's word; Jesus healed, so that we might be a healing presence; comes as God's message of mercy and grace for the broken world, a message of reconciliation, that we might have a ministry of reconciliation in a broken and lonely world. God is with us—*Emmanuel*—that we might be with our neighbors and friends, with coworkers and strangers, children and families, embodying God's love and peace, offering a living invitation to anyone who would be a part of it.

God was in Christ and Christ is in us, clay that we ourselves are. Methodist, Baptist, Presbyterian, Roman, Greek, Catholic, Orthodox, Reformed, Episcopal, clay, all of us with feet of clay and brains of clay. At least that is the way it feels to me many days, that my brain is just clay, that my heart is hard, dry clay. We are earthen vessels, clay pots, imperfect and leaky jars, but Christ is in us.

God was in Christ and Christ is among us.

Each of us, all of us: the flesh of God's Word, members of Christ's body. God's hands and feet and heart and tongue. Pieces of Christ glowing with the peace of Christ. Worshiping, praying, living *otherwise*.

Together.

———————— • ————————

I began in the Holy Land. Let me conclude there.

The second night in Israel, our group went to the Golan Volcanic Park. High up in the Golan Heights—a mountain range near Mount

Hermon, an area Israel took from Syria during the Six-Day War and Syria wants back—the park is part of the "disputed territories."

We went up the mountain in the evening, when, in the Hebrew way of thinking, the new day begins. But as we exited the bus we were chilled, not only with the evening mountain breeze, but also with the realities and reminders of the old days that were everywhere around us.

We sat in a little amphitheater built onto the side of the mountain and still in Israel, but as we looked east, not too far away, a few miles maybe, but quite visible, we saw the lights of a Syrian town—one of the places where the antigovernment unrest in Syria began, the attempt to topple the government of Bashar al-Assad.

From that distance the lights were beautiful, twinkling in the deepening dusk, and we could easily imagine couples eating dinner on the street or families playing games before bed—maybe music and dancing in the houses, parties, and those kinds of things.

Our guide told us that the people in that town live in abject terror day to day, night to night, with unceasing fear of government repression and reprisals. People disappear every day from that town because of political intrigue.

Meanwhile, above and behind us was what appeared to my admittedly untrained eye an incredibly sophisticated military outpost, a watching and listening station: all sorts of radar and antennae, and all the soldiers there on high alert, I am sure, with Syria so close and so unsettled.

Just below us, down the mountain and a little to our right, we saw great round disks. We quickly determined they were missile silos, death at the ready should they be needed.

And there we were, in between all of that: a group of fifty-four Christian tourists beset by missiles and military and militants (I guess you could call some of the people in that town, or revolutionaries) and within a rock's throw of what might have been nuclear warheads. We were strangers in that strange land, trying to understand all we were seeing and feeling.

We read some scripture—it was getting very dark by now—and then we began to sing: "Let there be peace on earth, and let it begin with me. . . ." A perfectly naive little song, but what else can you sing or hope or pray in such a moment? . . . "Let this be the moment now."

And right about then we heard a bomb from somewhere over there, a good ways away, but a bomb. And then automatic weapon's fire. AK-47, I guess.

All around us evidence of our warring madness, our division and isolation.

We looked over toward the blast, . . . and we kept singing.

We kept singing that song, praying that prayer, hoping that hope . . . let there be peace on earth. Each of us praying but together. So may this present darkness give way to that new day and all our isolated loneliness to reconciliation and peace.

Summary

Christians are called into community: to be a family in the house of prayer. There are dividing and shearing forces in the world, working to separate and divide us one against the other, and even in the church. Our mission, should we choose to accept it, is to learn once again how to pray and live together *otherwise*. Formed as a people, transformed by Word and Table, worship and mission, we invite others to join us in a community of joy where the many are one, and the one are many.

Questions for Reflection

1. How does a "communal" understanding of the gospel (a) encourage you, (b) challenge you, (c) frighten you?
2. In what areas do you see yourself, your church, your denomination as converted by the culture of individualism?

2

THE PROMISE OF PRAYER

Our life and our death is with our neighbor.
If we gain our brother, we have gained God, but if we scandalize
our brother, we have sinned against Christ.

ABBA ANTHONY

I was once interviewed by Debra Maffett, who was Miss America 1983. I was a guest on *The Harvest Show*, which Ms. Maffett cohosted at the time, there to talk about a book I had written.[1] That one show was my one and only stop on my one and only "book tour"!

The premise of the book is simple: that the narrative arc of the Christian year—the liturgical seasons of the church's worship—helps us better understand the "seasons" of Jesus' life and ministry and thereby interpret the "seasons" of our own discipleship. Lent, for instance, is the season to remember that for Jesus to be both King of the Jews (which we proclaim during the Twelve Days of Christmas) and Savior of the world (our message during Epiphany, the season following Christmas), Jesus will face increasing resistance, betrayal by his friends, personal isolation, anguished prayer, physical suffering, and finally death. The faithful suffering and death of Jesus is answered in turn by God's faithfulness to Jesus (which is the message of Easter). Annually reiterating Jesus' sufferings and God's vindication encourages us in the midst of our own faithful difficulties and teaches us that faith and suffering are not antithetical. Quite the contrary, in fact.

I was making the point in the interview that the narrative tradition of our faith in its historic liturgical expression has the power to *form* us as disciples and to *transform* both our perspectives and our living. I suggested that the idolatry of the age is individualism and that the gospel has been co-opted by this individualistic perspective. The consequence is the vanity of vanities: that faith and prayer exist in large part to enlist God in service to "my life and work" in the world. Alternatively, a more corporate, sacramental, and liturgical (and historic!) understanding of Christian life and worship would help discover, primarily, God's will for the world and, derivatively, our place alongside others as a part of that greater work.

Ms. Maffett was having none of it. She was polite to me (on camera), but she rejected the kind of spiritual formation I was advocating. Our last exchange went something like this:

MS. MAFFETT: *Maybe it should not be unusual to think this way, . . . but how do you make that leap? I mean, I've got so many friends, who you see in one phase of the walk or another phase, who can spend so many years, even decades, going through this because maybe their church does that, and it becomes just a lifeless ritual; to someone else you meet, Christ is alive in them. What do you say to that?*

MR. STEAGALD (after hesitating only a moment): *I guess I would compare it to singing hymns. When we sing the great hymns of the church, those are not words we have written. And there may be some people, I guess, who can sing those hymns without heart, or soul, or vitality . . . but for many people, those words, written by someone else, become in the singing of them their own testimony of faith.*

That little conversation evidences and proves the dilemma—and indeed the false dichotomy—that exists in many of our churches. In a WEIRD culture and in those churches where the prevailing culture holds sway, individual spirituality overtakes and overpowers the communal. Collaterally, the tradition is beaten, robbed, left beside the road as if dead.

Ancient and Modern Despair

There are few descriptions of isolation and despair more powerful than Job's. The mind and heart both nod and recoil at the stark images of anguish and isolation:

> *Today also my complaint is bitter. . . .*
> *Oh, that I knew where I might find him,*
>   *that I might come even to his dwelling!*
> *I would lay my case before him,*
>   *and fill my mouth with arguments.*
> (Job 23:2-4)

Job wants dialogue, conversation, even a trial if all other communication fails, where he can make his case. God might not answer or agree but at least there would be the satisfaction of having spoken the truth of experience, and the deeper hope that God would hear. And if God were just, God would also acquit.

But God is absent. Job says,

> *If I go forward, he is not there;*
>   *or backward, I cannot perceive him;*
> *on the left he hides, and I cannot behold him;*
>   *I turn to the right, but I cannot see him. . . .*
> *If only I could vanish in darkness,*
>   *and thick darkness would cover my face!*
> (Job 23:8-9, 17)

"If only I could vanish in darkness," Job says, meaning if only he could vanish in the same way God seems to have vanished! If darkness would cover my face as darkness covers God's!

This is the utter isolation and loneliness of a man who has lost everything: his children, his wife (in many ways), his friends (who are more concerned to be right than to be comforting), his health and property, and also his God. Job has lost any sense of community or connection. He is absolutely, to his own mind and experience, on his own, and he is feeling the incurable weight of his loneliness.

I wonder if Job is expressing the dark shadow of our own "enlightenment," the grim consequence of our prevailing culture of autonomous and atomized self?

I wonder if Job voices what many—preachers and people alike—feel and experience even in our own day? Without God, for whatever reason, but also without community—disconnected, disengaged, and weary with the loneliness.

———— • ————

To discuss the promise of prayer—that praying together, like singing together, turns "I" into "we," the first person singular into first person plural—is to articulate something about *why* we need prayer's promise.

Jonathan Haidt has persuaded me that hyperindividualism is not only the WEIRD culture in which we find ourselves, but the inevitable conclusion of the Enlightenment/American project (and Ayn Rand its patron saint!). In such a culture we may embrace temporary, volitional alliances—political or otherwise—or embody a narrow (if sometimes militant) clannishness; but the real message of our culture's "alternative gospel"[2] is that "I" (and the narrowest "we") is the most important lens for viewing any reality.

From this perspective persons are (ideally) self-reliant and self-sustaining, their own advocates—free in and unto themselves to make their own choices, build wealth, and create for themselves the "good life." Self-improvement, self-actualization, self-help, self-transformation: these are the ways and means of the American dream.

Pressed, however, this perspective is quite at odds with the gospel, and not only politically or ethically. Our culture's emphases have corrupted even our notions of "salvation" or "abundant life," should we think in such terms: whether salvation is considered a "this-world prosperity," thanks to a specific program or steps that grant "your best life now,"[3] or a "next-world security," based on your personal decision to accept Jesus as your Savior—in either case the whole matter is intensely personal and individualistic (read: selfish).[4]

In whatever form, the fruits of this "gospel of individualism"—either "I am my own alone," or "I am only *on* my own"—are inevitably blighted, withered by isolation and/or despair. And in either case, the presupposition of such an understanding counters the nature of the gospel Jesus preached and the nerve of the church Jesus founded. Jesus called individuals; but he called them into relationship, even when that meant their having to sacrifice deeply held political beliefs in order to follow him *together* (a Zealot *and* a tax collector? *Both* of them disciples of the same Teacher? Yes).

Whatever gifts the Holy Spirit gives to each, God intends for the benefit of all.

Pieces of Christ and the Peace of Christ

As a part of worship wherever I serve, we observe what is traditionally called the *Pax Christi*, the "Peace of Christ." The phrase comes from Paul: "Let the peace of Christ rule in your hearts, since as members of one body you were called to peace" (Col. 3:15, NIV). And so we take time, after the collect and the Doxology, to move here and there about the sanctuary, saying to our spiritual brothers and sisters, "The peace of Christ."

Not everyone likes it. I have heard criticisms ranging from "The Introit and gospel reading set a worshipful tone, and suddenly we are up and moving around, talking. It breaks the mood!" to "Why do you want me to shake hands with people? Who knows if they have sanitized?" One man used to say, "The same woman hugs me every week, and I don't even *like* her!" There are all sorts of reasons to keep our distance from people we know and more so from strangers. Even in worship some of us may not want to be "touching close" to anyone else at all. All of us, people as well as pastors, have found ways to hide, to practice our isolation, even in church.[5]

Still, despite the criticisms, as the shepherd of the flock I insist we share the peace of Christ. There are certain things worth fighting over. And I keep teaching: what we are doing is *practicing* hospitality, giving one another the gift that has been given us. If we can learn to do that among ourselves, we will be equipped to do it more and better in the world.

One day a member of our congregation, a young mother who along with her husband and children were relatively new believers and very new members of our church, told me that the previous Sunday, when I announced the *Pax Christi*, her son turned to her and said, "What am I supposed to do with a 'piece of Christ'?"

The phrase has haunted me ever since. "A piece of Christ."

Paul says in 1 Corinthians 12:27: "Now you are Christ's body and individual parts of it" (ISV). We not only *share* the peace of Christ, in other words, but we are pieces *of* the Christ—and like him, gathered together, broken for the world, and gathered together again.

———— • ————

One morning I was praying over the familiar scripture of Jesus' feeding the five thousand men. I was not praying alone: I sat among a roomful of pastors, some with heads bowed, some with chins raised, many with hands opened to receive whatever God would give us. A young woman walked us through the steps of *lectio divina*, that ancient practice of scripture reading. She read slowly, meditatively. She paused here and there to let a word, or the silence, sink in. She gave us, and the text gave us, and the Holy Spirit, we believe, gave us, time and space: to hear ourselves breathe, to hear our hearts beat, to listen for the still small voice of God.

I have read this story so many times, in one or the other of its four forms. It is the only miracle recorded by all four Gospels, and so worshipers come, sit before it regularly, to let it teach us. Most often we clergy grab a quick morsel and move on; which is to say, we just preach it again from one predictable aspect or another: we are the befuddled disciples who do not know what to do in the face of the many, but we do as we are told with what we have and somehow everyone gets fed.

Or we are the little boy, giving what we have been given, what we have been saving for ourselves, and somehow everyone gets fed.

Or we are Jesus, sort of, with compassion for the crowds, maybe, or not so much compassion, but we tell everyone to sit and we pray over what we have been given, and somehow everyone gets fed.

We rarely highlight this remarkable fact: that in the face of the hungry crowd, Jesus took what was handed to him and *gave thanks for it.*[6]

Yeah, you know, whatever.

But that day, sitting before the text, I received something different. I heard a different voice, and not a loud voice—just still and small—but insistent too and incessant, demanding to be heard. And what I heard was something I had never thought before.

What if I am the bread? Or the fish? Or piece of either, an ingredient or morsel? And others like me likewise? And not much of me, but whatever I am, just a plain barley loaf or a dried fish but part of what has been given to Jesus either by my parents' prayers or my own volition? And Jesus takes me, just as I am, and others with me, just as they are, and he prays over us and parts us and distributes us to the crowds? So that other hungry souls can be fed.

I can see that. Feel that too.

But what if, on the other side of Jesus' praying and giving, I am "leftovers," scraps cast aside when the crowd is sated? A piece of the piece that I was at the beginning? Just a crust? And maybe the crowds have eaten up the best part of me, so that there is nothing much left to be done with me but to be cast on the ground, away?

Bur Jesus says, "Gather up all the pieces, so that nothing is lost" (see John 6:12).

And so the disciples gather up the pieces, the scraps and crusts, collect them into twelve baskets. And anyone who knows anything about scripture knows that "twelve" always refers, one way or the other, to the people of God, the children of Abraham, the disciples—Jesus says that what is left at the end of the meal, even the little pieces, is also to be saved.

Maybe that is what happens every week, Sunday by Sunday: we are gathered together again as the people of God, so that Jesus can receive us and pray over us and distribute us again into the hungry world. Maybe that is the story of discipleship and ministry, always: our lives and the pieces of our lives, distributed, recollected, distributed again. And all that is left of us day to day, week to week, life to life, is a crust. That is the way it feels sometimes. "But the crust is where all the nutrients are," says a friend.

"Yes, but the crust is what most people cut off or throw away."

But Jesus does not and will not. He commands that even the pieces be gathered into his baskets, so that nothing of us is lost.

Individual Faith and Christian Belonging

The darkness that is upon our culture now is not just fragmentation but *disintegrated* fragmentation, the brokenness and exclusion that leaves us in *mere* pieces, alone, pitting us against one another. Whether as individuals or clans, whether politically or religiously, whether economically or ideologically, we are in pieces. Our faith and worship not only do not redeem our loneliness or overcome our divisions but in fact seem to deepen the divides.

And maybe it has always been so. But there has never been a time since Jesus when it *ought* to have been so, or a time when we more needed the alternative the church in its fullness may provide. There has never been a time when we more needed to see ourselves as pieces of Christ, needed each other to realize the fullness of the gospel and Christian life, so that together, we may begin to experience the peace of Christ.

Dr. Haidt is not a believer. And yet, in contrast to the "New Atheists," he speaks appreciatively of the value of religion, at least in terms of "identification" and, following Émile Durkheim, "the creation of a community."[7] He believes religion can have (though it does not always have) a positive social function in terms of hospitality, charitableness, and the like. Against those who would blithely dismiss the role and value of religious faith, he warns (as Durkheim did over a century ago) that societies depend on "shared moral matrices." While the full consequences of losing the "exoskeleton of religion" cannot yet be determined, the first indicators are grim.[8]

I am less concerned with the general sociological argument of Durkheim and Haidt than with its particular application to Christian life. Specifically, when we lose authentic community, our "exoskeleton" of identification and Christian practice—which is really not external at all but the most compelling aspect of the church's DNA: what Bonhoeffer called "life together" and Dr. King described as "the Beloved Community"—we lose the very entity Jesus established and into which he called us. If we lose incarnation to mere individualism, the body to its independent members, Christ will have lived and died to no earthly effect. If by our allegiance to the culture we help tear down the church Christ built up, we lose the embodied gospel, the continuing incarnation, and with them the transforming purpose and power of our faith.

It may be that we have already lost it. Perhaps most American Christians and churches are already too WEIRD to embrace, much less embody, the communal gospel Jesus preached or the body of Christ Paul envisioned. Tragically, if the *faithful* are unconverted and unconvinced *by our own evangel*, we are of all people most to be pitied: unable to see the depth of our plight[9] and oblivious to the transforming joy of real community, just like the servants at the wedding in Cana of Galilee. At that party, everyone and everything *except* the servants was changed by the presence and power of Jesus.

The wine, of course. And it may be that the water Jesus turned into wine was the water in the stone jars. Or it may be that it was the well itself that was changed. For textual and theological reasons, that was the opinion of my college New Testament professor.

The disciples too were changed, odd as that sounds. They were already following Jesus, but when they saw the sign, they "believed in him" (John 2:11). If it is bad and scary news that followers and even disciples can be *un*believers, it is good news indeed that, then and now, followers and disciples can be changed.

The steward too was changed: his mood, at least, because the party was saved!

But the servants? They were unchanged. Note well: They were there at the party. They did what Jesus told them to do. They even knew what had happened . . . but they said nothing. They enjoyed nothing. And nobody so much as thanked Jesus for his wedding present to the couple because the servants said nothing either to declare or to interpret the sign.

The servants are "the church," aware but unchanged. Obedient but joylessly silent.

The hope is that as we keep coming to the party, as we see what we have not always experienced, as we begin to proclaim and come to enjoy what others before us have rejoiced to receive—and as we more fully recognize the struggle we are in, begin to engage in those practices that can turn the tide—we will not only proclaim "doctrine" but become the proof of what we preach.

The Holy, Catholic, and Apostolic Church

Henri Nouwen once wrote that the gospel "doesn't just contain *ideas* worth remembering. It is a *message* responding to our individual human *condition*" and that doctrines—Christian doctrines—"are not alien formulations which we must adhere to but the documentation of the most profound human experiences which, transcending time and place, are handed over from generation to generation as a light in our darkness."[10]

While Protestants don't much believe the doctrine of transubstantiation, considering it one of those "alien formulations," I am not so sure but that maybe we ought to rethink. The doctrine of transubstantiation says basically this: We offer to God ordinary things—bread, wine, or Welch's—and we pray over them. What we see after the prayers looks the same: the bread like bread; the wine or juice like wine or juice. But where our eyes can't see, God has changed the *substance* of that bread and wine, has made it into the Body and Blood of Christ.

That is what happens to us when we pray: we offer ourselves to God, ordinary folk that we are, and deep below the surface of things we are changed, are being changed from fragmented individuals into a family, from atomized selves into the church. We do not lose our God-given distinctiveness, only our desolating isolation. By praying in community we become a community; we are changed from no people into God's people: the body of Christ, the flesh of God's word, the continuing incarnation of Jesus. We are fitted for the work that is ours and take our place in the great redemption story, to advance the ministry of healing and reconciliation that is so near God's heart.

That is not an abstract doctrine to which we may or may not adhere, but the deepest expression of who we are empowered to be as disciples. Our profoundest experience as humans is to be pieces of Christ, offering to others the peace of Christ.

Against the heresies of selfishness and the despair of isolation, the church proclaims a deep and abiding unity, the peace of Christ, one that is given and that in turn must be continually shared—and is thereby achieved. That is the promise of praying together.

We are all children of God, and by praying the Our Father and other transformational prayers, we become family. As family, no one is in a position to disdain a brother or sister, rich or poor, for we are brothers and sisters *at all* because we claim the Father as *ours*. As members together of the family, we are called to shoulder our share of the community's needs, to use our individual gifts for the benefit of all, to give more than we receive.

The Children of Light Lost in the Darkness

Saint Paul writes to the Christians in Colossae that God "has rescued us from the dominion of darkness," has "qualified [us] to share in the inheritance of his holy people in the kingdom of light" (Col. 1:13, 12, NIV). It is a beautiful image, and the theological reality of God's will and purposes. In fact, however, the church is often as lost in the darkness as others. One aspect of that darkness is well described by Dean Obeidallah, a former attorney and now political humorist.

In an incisive piece for CNN, Mr. Obeidallah suggests that we live in an era of "Instant Outrage." "Never," he says, "have so many been so outraged by so little."[11] In the old days, he says, if something offended you, you had to write a letter, put the letter in an envelope, stamp the envelope, put it in the mail, wait three days for it to arrive—then double the time to hear back, if you ever did—but it gave you time to simmer down.

Now, with Twitter, Facebook, e-mail forwarding and the like (and no matter, really, if what you are forwarding has any basis in real fact), you can lay your outrage out there for everyone immediately to see and to feed off everyone else's. And in any given day, in any given news cycle, in the unending eternity of a given news week, somebody is outraged about something all the time.

Obeidallah says that our instant outrage is, among other things, distracting—and *distraction* is another word for "acedia," for sloth, for losing focus. We get bitten by *that* dragon head, get distracted, and lose focus. He notes that by some accounts, 22 percent of all children are living in poverty, but instead of moving with abandon to help a child in need, we have heated debate about what constitutes poverty or where the poverty line actually is.

We are distracted by our instant outrage, but our culture does not leave it at that. We have been taught to nurse the distraction, to deepen the divisions. And so the problem is not simply instant outrage but old grudges. And easy offense. And gross insensitivity. And impatience. And hot-button politics. There are so many things to divide us, so many things to distance us, to make us bite and devour one another, as Paul says in Galatians 5, that on a given Sunday none of us may feel, much less pass, the peace of Christ.

The fruit of the Spirit may be love, joy, peace, patience, kindness, goodness, faithfulness, gentleness, and self-control—but that fruit is often blighted by the radioactivity of our contentious culture. The gospel teaches forgiveness, forbearance, long-suffering, deference, humility, and peacemaking, but the present darkness threatens to swallow those points of light. And it will if the peacemakers and the forgiving grope through the darkness alone.

But those who follow Jesus are pledged to one another, and when the culture does its divide-and-conquer thing we are privileged and empowered to live *otherwise*—with no pride or greed or lust or despair or any of the many other things (like instant outrage) that drive wedges between us.

But how do we do that? How do we live otherwise? Or begin to live that way?

One Friday night I took our confirmation class to the synagogue for shabbat. We went to the later service at eight o'clock p.m. It was not well-attended, though the place had been packed at six. The cantor and the rabbi were clearly tired and had trouble getting started: they couldn't get the sabbath candles lit; there was some issue with the PowerPoint; everything was just a little out of sync. We, with them, were struggling.

But the leaders kept at it. They kept singing, even when the pianist missed a beat. They kept praying, even when worshipers were having difficulty finding the page. Their tenacity seemed to suggest that sabbath itself is always more important than how her children manage to observe it. There seemed to be an underlying conviction that if they kept singing, they would eventually find the rhythm. If they kept praying, they would experience the presence of God. If they kept trying to worship, even if they weren't *feeling* it, they might actually find themselves worshiping.

And I think they did. But even if they had not, the service was not about them and their feelings but about God and God's praise.

I find myself thinking that we too are to say our prayers even when we don't feel like praying them: the Psalter, the Jesus Prayer, the collects and confessions. These ancient words are the handles to our pump, get the living water to the surface. These words are the primers to our surrender. We give ourselves to the language of prayer so that prayer, real prayer, may be given to us.

And we determine to pray together so that when one of us falters, others are there to pick us up. So that when we are outraged, or prideful, we have friends to remind us who we are beneath all that. And in Whose family we are.

Promise and Provision

In Mark's Gospel we read:

> *The apostles gathered around Jesus and reported to him all they had done and taught. Then, because so many people were*

coming and going that they did not even have a chance to eat, he said to them, "Come with me by yourselves to a quiet place and get some rest." So they went away by themselves in a boat to a solitary place. But many who saw them leaving recognized them and ran on foot from all the towns and got there ahead of them. When Jesus landed and saw a large crowd, he had compassion on them, because they were like sheep without a shepherd. So he began teaching them many things. (Mark 6:30-34, NIV)

Jesus had given his disciples power to do mighty work; Jesus had also prepared them for rejection and given instructions as to how they were to behave *when* rejected. They had gone out. They had come back. And when they came back they brought with them reports "of all they had done and taught."

And then Jesus took them away by themselves, just them and Jesus, so that all of them could rest awhile. It is a picture of sabbath for Christians, a time for rest in the presence of Jesus—the peace of Christ.

There were many more people to be healed; very soon, they would be back at work because people from everywhere followed them and surrounded them and reached out to get a piece of them, to find healing and peace from them. . . .

But here there was a moment of sabbath, of rest, of time away for the disciples.

As Jesus' disciples, the eventual result of sabbath is that we will be energized, centered, and empowered to do God's work in the world. But the necessary prerequisite to sabbath is that we come away from what we have been doing and come back to Jesus. Think of it as the first gesture, the first movement of prayer. We set aside our busyness, leave behind our obligations, cease and desist thinking so many other scattering thoughts that we might be gathered again to the heart of Jesus. As Tony Campolo and Mary Darling put it, "These times of silence [help] us find the inner peace in Christ that equips us to bring peace to others."[12]

When we are able to take those few moments, to be silent with one another before God, we find both our work and our energy for that work: a way to speak peace and peace enough to speak it. And blessed, Jesus said, are the peacemakers.

We come to Jesus, together, away from the tasks to which he has assigned us, and into his presence. We see the beauty of his presence, feel the power of his promises, experience peace away from the clamor. We share with him our hearts, and he shares with us his will, helps us discern God's spirit in others, readies us to return.

We come away from others for a while to see them *really*, so as to come back to serve them as if we were serving Christ, until that day when we shall all come to him and find with him and in him that final rest, that final praise, sabbath for the world and all its children.

We need not be the last to experience or enjoy what God is doing—like the servants in Cana: doing what we are told, our work and our duty—but at the end unconverted. Observing but not experiencing. At the party but unchanged.

Rather, we are summoned now, together, to be with Jesus, to eat with him and drink that "already" wine, a foretaste of the feast God has prepared for all people.

Summary

The promise of prayer together is the promise of community: across time and all the divides we are graced to become the body of Christ. Isolation and death give way to connection and life, as Paul's image of the body implies. The culture wants us divided and at odds; the gospel calls us together—each and all. As we become the family of God, living in the house of prayer, we experience more and more of the gift Jesus has lived and died to give us.

Questions for Reflection

1. How does being one member in the body of Christ contrast with the culture's message, and how does reclaiming that goal challenge you and/or your church?

2. Does your congregation "pass the peace"? How does passing the peace differ from saying good morning to your neighbor?

3

THE PEOPLE OF PRAYER

God is able to save those who in this life never belonged to his Church.
But, looking at the matter from our *side, this does not entitle any*
of us to say, "The Church is unnecessary for me." . . . The Christian
is the one who has brothers and sisters. He belongs to a family—
the family of the Church.

BISHOP KALLISTOS WARE

M y bags had been long packed. I was waiting for Terry and Laurel.
We would gather up my son Jacob on the way and ride together
to the airport: Greensboro to Philadelphia, Philadelphia to Tel Aviv—
winging our way through the darkness toward the sabbath sun.

For a year we had been planning this trip. The truth is that for
my whole life I had longed to make such a pilgrimage: to see the
Galilee and Caesarea, to pray at the Mount of Olives and the Western Wall. To see where Jesus preached and taught, to pray where
he worshiped and died. To breathe the air he breathed and feel the
waters of his baptism on my own flesh. To board a boat as his disciples did, to look for his coming on the sea he calmed, and perhaps
more than once.

Into those same unpredictably turbulent but unfailingly obedient waters, Jesus commanded Peter, feckless and incredulous, to
let down his nets for a catch. Neither Peter nor any of the other

— 53 —

fishermen-disciples Jesus called ever caught so much as a single fish unless Jesus guided them. But when he did, and perhaps more than once, the vaulted deeps gave so much treasure that Peter and the others could not get the net to shore, feared their boat might sink.

And now, finally, my family and I were going. His place would be my place, at least for a while. I hoped to receive his peace as my peace: the peace of Christ in the place of Christ. I would be a stranger in a strange land to be sure, but I felt for all the world as if I were on my way home, my truest earthly home, this eternally holy land. Lo, I had waited these many years to walk where Jesus walked, to see where Jesus worked, to feel the holy dust of that Holy Land on my unholy face. To be covered in my Rabbi's dust: my life's goal and travel itinerary. And I prayed that should tears come, it would please the Lord to smear the dust and my tears like a holy paste on my eyes, that I might see the glory God has prepared for all earth's children.

I too am one of those for whom that glory is prepared, but I am not alone: God's glory has been prepared for all his people. God prepares the people for glory. We have been wired with a deep and abiding hope: to see the promises of God fulfilled, to see the kingdom come, on earth as it is in heaven.

While I waited for my friends I watched an old video, over and over again.[1] It is a rare clip, black and white, shot in Jerusalem in 1925. Our guide for the trip, who sent the link to our tour host to share with us, observed that much of the old city is unchanged since the video was made. Except, it occurred to me to think, that all of the people in the video are dead. This is no small point: all the peasants, rabbis, pilgrims, and priests: dead.

Transfixed, I watched them pray at the Western Wall. Some stood still; some rocked;[2] some knelt. Some held prayer books, read aloud. Some were empty-handed and silent. One lady had her hands on the lower stones, tracing her fingers over the ancient Hebrew inscriptions.

Yes, the people in the clip are all dead; but the hopes of God's people live on in that eternal city, unchanged from David to Solomon, from 1925 to Revelation 21. The film spoke powerfully to me who would soon hope to pray some of those same prayers in some of those same places. I acknowledged that while *those* particular pray-ers are gone, the prayers continue to be prayed without ceasing, in unbroken line. The invitation *to pray*, to pray *together*, is never withdrawn: "Seek ye my face!" (see Ps. 27:8, KJV). Our hearts answer, "Thy face, LORD, will I seek." And so we do. We come, geographically, sometimes, but spiritually and confessionally too, with our ancestors and elders, our brothers and sisters, our children and their children and their children after them.

We too rock a bit, whether in joy or sorrow, hope or dread. We find ourselves kneeling as well, as if to press our own souls' fingers into the ancient words of covenant carved deep into the foundations of our faith. We stand still. We wait on the Lord. We believe that God continues to hear. And we believe that God continues to answer. Not fully, not yet; and perhaps because the prayers have not all been prayed. Not fully, not yet.

Some Jews believe that when the sabbath is faithfully celebrated, Messiah will finally come. Those of us who believe Messiah has already come continue faithfully to pray for the sabbath: rest for our souls and final rest for the world to celebrate.

The Atheist/Apologist

Jonathan Haidt dismisses the New Atheists' vision of religion as too simple by half. He notes that religion has social worth and evolutionary merit, though he also seems to believe that eventually the need for religion, perhaps like the need for an appendix, will disappear. Still, his secularist appreciation for religion's *social* function cracks the realm of modern skepticism to allow at least a bit of the numinous to seep in.

And even if Haidt imagines that "our ability to believe in supernatural agents may well have begun as an accidental by-product of a hypersensitive agency detection device," he adds that "once early humans began believing in such agents, the groups that used them to construct moral communities were the ones that lasted and prospered."[3]

In other words, if religion is studied merely as "a set of beliefs about supernatural agents, and these beliefs are said to be the cause of a wide range of harmful actions," then the *social function* of religion is ignored. Haidt contends that "the function of [religious] beliefs and practices is *ultimately to create a community*."[4] Further, "*the very ritual practices that the New Atheists dismiss as costly, inefficient, and irrational turn out to be a solution to one of the hardest problems humans face: cooperation without kinship.*"[5]

At a functional level, the point Haidt makes is that faith serves the community by creating and fostering and reinforcing community. "Irrational beliefs [his term] can sometimes help the group function *more rationally*, particularly when those beliefs rest upon the Sanctity foundation. *Sacredness binds people together.*"[6]

I among others have long maintained that the inarguable critique of some religious behavior by the New Atheists—fundamentalism's intolerances, inquisitions, and terrorism—does not do justice to a vast other body of religious behavior—the founding of hospitals, schools, colleges; the feeding of the needy, medical missions, and the like.

Daniel Dennett, conversely, has written that "you don't get to advertise all the good that your religion does without first scrupulously subtracting all the harm it does and considering seriously the question of whether some other religion, or no religion at all, does better."[7] Fair enough. But Jonathan Haidt offers a withering reply to the question of "consequences." That is, how do we evaluate religious vs. nonreligious involvement in terms of community service, giving to charitable causes, and so on?[8] Citing the research of Robert Putnam and David Campbell, Haidt asks, "Why are religious people better neighbors and citizens?" His answer: "The only thing that was reliably and powerfully associated with the moral benefits of religion was *how enmeshed people were in relationships with their co-religionists.* It's the friendships and group activities, carried out within a moral matrix that emphasizes selflessness. That's what brings out the best in people." Haidt concludes, "Putnam and Campbell reject the New Atheist emphasis on belief and reach a conclusion straight out of

Durkheim: 'It is religious belongingness that matters for neighborliness, not religious believing.'"[9]

I have quoted Dr. Haidt often; I am not trying to summarize his work or offer a book review, but I am interested to hear a thoroughgoing secularist acknowledge, describe, and diagnose the deep isolations of our culture and its deeply isolating agendas. Even more, in Dr. Haidt we hear a nonbeliever offer what we might go so far as to call "testimony" to the psychological, practical, and even numinous power of "life together." If responsible nonbelievers can trumpet the value of prayer- and practice-formed community, how ironic it is that American Christians are not only mostly ignorant of but even unconverted by our own gospel!

The book of Ephesians anticipates and praises the Day, as indeed our story and sacraments both embody and point to the time when Christ will be "all in all" (1:23). Our practice of prayer and the story and sacraments that give rise to our prayers, are the eternity-honored means by which individuals, from wildly divergent backgrounds and beliefs, may be reformed and transformed into members of the one body of Christ. Praying together is the template that forms that community and the fuel that empowers it. In sum, the "mystic, sweet communion"[10] is a once-and-future reality evidenced among us even now—here and there, now and then.

Many fear such intimacy and dependence and not least some members of the church that proclaims it! The reasons for such fears are complex. Dr. Haidt suggests that in many individuals, many isolationists, many hate groups, many nations, the fear of deeper community is born out of what appears to be a vestigial "tribal configuration" that demands the assimilation or destruction of those who are not "like we are."[11] That, or hide from them, even when they are in the next pew! Evolutionarily, subconsciously, we are only more or less "narrowly groupish."

Be that as it may developmentally or psychologically, the church exists theologically, historically, and spiritually to *break down* the barriers between us; and, where there used to be "two or more," whether people or groups, to make us "one" people. The love of enemies, rather than the killing or subjugating of them, and the embrace of ever more "others," births the kind of community that fosters "cooperation without kinship." Or perhaps an entirely new kind of kinship is birthed.

The One, Holy, Catholic Church

Early in my ministry I determined to close every worship service I led with the Apostles' Creed. The rationale was this: whether the sermon "speaks" or not; whether the hymns thrill or befuddle; whether the scriptures resonate or drone; when, in other words, someone might be tempted to say we "got nothing" out of worship (thus betraying captivity to the culture, imagining that worship is about our gratification instead of God's glory), it is crucial to remember—and even more crucial at the end of those very kinds of services—who we are and Whom we serve. We are those who have been called and set apart. Once we were no people and now we are God's people, a royal priesthood by God's own choosing and ordaining (1 Pet. 2:9-10). God calls, and so we answer, each and all of us together: "I believe in God, the Father Almighty. . . . I believe in Jesus Christ, his only Son, our Lord. . . . I believe in the Holy Spirit. . . ."

And "I believe in . . . the holy catholic church." It is a startling confession: to believe in the church at all, much less that the church is holy. Or that it is *catholic*. More than occasionally I catch heat: that we say the Creed so much and that I do my best to make sure we say "catholic" instead of "Christian" or "universal."

One of my congregants, a former Lutheran, a dour and sour woman who had spent her life working in a mayonnaise factory, adding vinegar to the egg whites—and I always kind of thought maybe that was what did it to her—refused to say the word *catholic*. She said, "holy Christian church," which was okay theologically but defeated the purpose *liturgically*.

I explained that when it is capitalized *Catholic*, we are speaking of the Roman Church, but that when it is spelled with a lowercase *c*, the word means universal, all-inclusive, global, cosmic, diffuse, eclectic, ecumenical, but she would not relent. Everyone else says *catholic* and perhaps some mean *Catholic*, but the reason we say the Creed at all is to break down barriers, not erect them; to form the community: the "I," taken together with all other "I's," is what makes and shapes the "we" of the congregation. I said that by setting herself apart in that way, by disrupting both the rhythm and the uniformity of the Creed, she disrupted the community we were trying to form. Alas.

But, yes, we believe in the universal, all-inclusive, global, cosmic, Christian, and catholic church. I try to communicate, in preaching and worship, in teaching and pastoral care, what John Wesley called the "catholic spirit," whereby we affirm that "what has been believed everywhere, always, and by everyone"[12] is what we believe too.

That is not just an *idea* worth remembering. It is a *message* responding to our *condition*. Not an alien formulation to which we must adhere but a documentation of the most profound human experiences and a proclamation of the most profound hope and vision of our faith: all people in their proper place with one another and before God. That message transcends time and place, even as it is "handed over from generation to generation as a light in our darkness."[13]

The darkness of our age is the kind of individualism and narrow tribalism that fractures and fragments society and often even the church. The light we are handing on is the documentation, the profound experience of One who has died that we might be one. This gospel transcends time and place and preference.

And so we say the Creed, confess that we believe in the church, the whole church, and that all who believe in Jesus are a part of it. We believe in the whole and the holy catholic church. These are not merely words; this is no mere idea or alien formulation. It is indeed a documentation of our most profound human experience and hope.

If pressed to explain, one of my own "documentary" reasons for saying "holy catholic church" is this: Several years ago I got a phone call from my supervisor. The night before, the pastor of a congregation near the one I served had been arrested at the airport for solicitation and was immediately suspended. The supervisor assigned pastoral responsibility for the stricken and suddenly shepherdless congregation to me.

A HOUSE of PRAYER

———— • ————

Two days after that tragedy, word came to me that a young woman in my "new" congregation had turned a .22 long rifle to her belly and killed herself. By all accounts she was a sweet but troubled soul, restless and unsure of her place in the world. She evidenced her angst and anger with elaborate tattoos and body piercings. She drifted from school to school and job to job, all the while numbing herself with alcohol and chemicals. One afternoon, sitting in her car in her parents' driveway, a final, irrational panic seized her.

The young woman's suicide rocked the whole community and put me in an almost impossible pastoral situation. I did not know the family. I had never been in the sanctuary of that church. I was not familiar with their social webbing or "local" traditions. In a panic of my own I called my supervisor and demanded that the suspended pastor be allowed to tend to this situation, no matter the scandal or tragedy that had overtaken him. He had been there for years. The family was pleading for his ministrations. My arguments did not prevail. I would have to offer pastoral care to a family I did not know, in the midst of a horror I could not begin to comprehend.

The young woman's name was Eve, of all things. I made my fearful way to the house with no idea what to say to her family in the face of all the losses they had suffered—not only their daughter, but their pastor and friend, and maybe their God too. I had no clue how to step into that darkness with them, much less represent the very God they may well have blamed. What word might I offer? I had no such word.

Eyes swollen, jaw set, the mother asked me first thing if it would be all right with me (she was asking about *my* feelings!) if they asked the Lutheran pastor who had baptized Eve to do the funeral sermon.

"Absolutely," I said to her. (I was so relieved I barely had breath to reply.)

"Thank you," she said to me. ("Thank you, Jesus," I whispered to the Holy One.)

On that funeral day, the United Methodist sanctuary was packed with its members, but there were many area Pentecostals and Catholics in attendance too. I read the scriptures, prayed the prayers. A Baptist girl wept out a solo. And then the Lutheran minister, vested

—— 60 ——

in the bright and beautiful raiment of his tradition, stood to bring us the Word of the Lord. And what he said was this:

"Long before Eve thought to end her life, God had deigned to grant her life. And long before she knew whether or not to choose God, God had already chosen her. And long before she first marked herself with tattoo ink or body jewelry—and she did those things to craft an identity for herself, an identity *against* so many other ideas and identities, as if to say, 'Hands off! Stay away! I'm alone!' all those tattoos like walls around her, 'No Trespassing' signs posted on the door of her heart—*long* before that, God had already marked her with the water of her baptism"—he raised his right hand high into the air to make the sign of the cross—"the watermark of God's grace, that reaches deeper than any ink."

He said, "Before she had rejected a thing, God had made her his own. The water of God's grace forever named her and claimed her. She was God's, and is God's, and will be God's. And now, in God's healing presence, at last Eve knows who she always was. A beloved child of God and at rest in the healing presence of God."

Earlier in the service I had read from Revelation 2:17: "Let anyone who has an ear listen to what the Spirit is saying to the churches. To everyone who conquers I will give some of the hidden manna, and I will give a white stone, and on the white stone is written a new name that no one knows except the one who receives it."

At least three traditions, not counting all the tributaries, were represented in that overflowing congregation. But one Lord, one faith, one baptism. One gospel; one comfort; and one holy, catholic, and apostolic succession—all of us standing under the authority and grace of ancient words made faith, ancient prayers made hope, abiding grief made into love. We were simultaneously beneficiaries and evidence of the great overarching and undergirding grace of the church. And all the people said, "Amen."

"Remember her baptism and be thankful." That is what that dear Lutheran priest said for that poor desperate girl.

"Remember their baptism and be thankful"—I have said that many times since, in sanctuaries and chapels and at gravesides. And if the dearly or not-so-dearly departed were not baptized, I have said,

"Remember that God's grace is expressed in the water but not limited to the water. With water or without, God claims us, and does not despise the affliction of the afflicted but desires that all God's children be well and at peace."

What I have said most often is this: "Remember *Jesus'* baptism and be thankful: that Jesus came to the Jordan, to take his place with us, to dwell among us and for us. His name, after all—one of his given names—is *Emmanuel*, 'God with us.'"

———————— • ————————

Jesus came to the Jordan to be baptized by John. Christians the world over remember that story about how John was preaching out by the Jordan River and all the people came to be baptized as a symbol of their repentance, their desire to be cleansed of their sins. And Jesus came too, which caused the church no small embarrassment later, when it told the story.

Jesus needed no repentance, so why would he come for baptism? Jesus was greater than John, so why would Jesus submit to John's authority? One can almost hear the early church's response echoed in John's protest. "It is I who need to be baptized by you," he said (see Matt. 3:13) and would have prevented Jesus from being baptized at all, but Jesus urged him and so John obediently consented.

It is a wondrous picture: Jesus standing shoulder to shoulder with the people he came to seek and serve and save. Emmanuel: God with them there in the water. And we who follow him into the water are ourselves baptized; we stand with him with them. Our baptism not only gives us name and hope: it gives us identity and purpose. Our baptism is not only promise but command. Our baptism not only cleanses us but unites us with everyone else who comes to the waters.

Oscar Romero was the archbishop of El Salvador who was assassinated in 1980 by, in all probability, a government death squad because he dared to stand with the poor against the rich, the powerful, and the connected. His stand with the poor even put him at odds with many other Catholic priests who regularly showed traditional, cultural favoritism toward the rich and granted special privilege to the powerful.

His stand put him at odds with his own family too.

In a film about the archbishop, titled simply *Romero*, the tension between him and all the powers that be is evidenced in an (apocryphal?) argument he has with his well-to-do goddaughter, who brings her child to him for baptism. She is horrified when Romero insists the child be baptized with all the other children. He reminds her that in baptism there is no distinction between persons, rich, poor, or otherwise; but she does not want her child baptized in the same water as the poor children. She wants a private baptism after the water in the font has been changed. And nothing unusual about her request: such was the custom and tradition in El Salvador.

Romero refused. He understood, rightly, that for Jesus to stand shoulder to shoulder with us in baptism means that in our baptisms, we stand shoulder to shoulder with him. We identify, take our place with those he came to seek and to serve and to save. In our baptisms, we are given not only the name of Christ, not only the promise of Christ, but the command and mission of Christ as well—to stand shoulder to shoulder with the people because we represent Jesus in the world.

We represent Jesus in the world.

Remember your baptism. Remember their baptisms. Remember Jesus' baptism. I say all that because we can sometimes forget or choose to forget what all our baptisms mean. The water is both grace and summons, blessing and call. Different as we are, we are one in Christ because of our baptism. This water names us, claims us, unites us.

Remember and be *thankful*. I say that too, because we are not always thankful to have been summoned to the water, not always happy about the consequence or obligations of baptism.

My friend Ron's son, Chris, after a tough day at school, when what he most wanted to do was punch a classmate or pop his head like a pimple—was reminded that he had to forgive him instead. "And *why* do I have to forgive him?" Chris asked. "Because you are a Christian," Ron said, "because you have been baptized."

"Where do I go to get *un*baptized?" Chris asked. Sometimes we would rather not remember our baptisms, and do not like to be reminded who we are.

Every time our congregation baptizes a child, in the middle of the liturgy I leave the font with the bowl in my hands and walk up and down the aisle, dipping my fingers into the water to sling it on folks left and right. Some people try to dodge the drops, don't like the feel of cold water on their bald spots or rouge. But I sling the water as insistently as I lead the Creed. It is an outrageous act, if you look at it one way, shocking and intrusive, more to be experienced than chosen. But it is no more outrageous, really, than pouring water on the head of an infant, naming that child with the name of Christ, as we ourselves were so named: Christian, little Christ.

That is what baptism is, essentially: a naming ceremony. A *naming* ceremony.

In former generations, and in some places and traditions still, the minister or priest takes the infant from the arms of its mother or father. The minister asks, "What name is given to this child?" and the parents respond, say out loud whatever name they have chosen . . . whatever name the child is to be given . . . the *given* name, the Christian name, even *baptismal* name, it is sometimes called, as opposed to the family name or surname . . . Thomas or Susan or Ann or Richard. Or Eve.

But there is another naming going on at that same baptismal moment; a deeper and more abiding naming, deeper than the name the parents give or the preacher calls out. There is a naming God is doing, a naming that will be written not only on the birth certificate or the church roll, but in the Lamb's own scrolls; a name that is to be carved not just into gray granite to mark death but into the white stone that signals life and identity and peace: the disciple's name, a true and lasting name, the name by which God has claimed and known that one.

What is revealed at the last is accomplished at the font. God claims, names, promises. Before we can choose God, God has already chosen us. Before we know to say yes to God, God says yes to us.

God names us with the name of the only Son, Jesus, and God promises to be with us as God was with him . . . all of that grace poured with the water onto the head of the one who is baptized.

That choosing, claiming, naming, and promising are crucial for us to remember, crucial for us to let that memory ground our thanks. Gathering around the font, flicking and being flicked by water, saying the Creed, we are *forcibly* reminded of who we are, Whose we are, and what we are: the family of God, brothers and sisters all, birthed and rebirthed every time we gather around the font.

We are the called, the commanded, the promised. And so it is appropriate and mandatory to be thankful, to reaffirm our vows to Christ, to celebrate that every time we are near the holy water we are shoulder to shoulder with Jesus, with one another and with the poor lost world Jesus loved so much.

Prayers and Promises, Longing and Faith

More than stones, the foundation of the Temple was prayer: The prayer of Solomon, of course, but all the prayers that preceded that prayer too.

The mortar of the church is prayer. And our prayer, joined to that of Solomon and every prayer prayed since, is that God will make "all things new," that God will make me new as well and all those who likewise have longed for and loved God's appearing. That we who pray to God will be made the people of God at last. That God may take up eternal residence, make eternal dwelling among us!

With our prayer books or empty handed, speaking or silent, on account of the tradition or in spite of it, we pray—and indeed all of humanity prays, whether they know it or not—to see the redemption God has promised; we pray to see the end of the old world and the beginning of the new, the demise of enmity in us and between us, the feast that God will prepare for *all* peoples.

Our eyes long to see the shroud taken away, the veil removed from all peoples. Our mouths are formed, our tongues thirst to say, "Lo, this is our God; we have waited for him, so that he might save us. This is the LORD for whom we have waited; let us be glad and rejoice in his salvation" (Isa. 25:9).

The world, we ourselves—in our hearts, relationships, ministries, politics—are or feel so dead and buried. For so long there has been about us a stench of lonely despair and islandated hopelessness. Our own hearts rail at Jesus much as Martha did. If he had *been here*, if he had not dallied or delayed but come when we needed him, we wouldn't be in this mess. Our spirits draw back from him as he seems to have drawn back from us, failing to come at our moment of greatest need. As Mary did, we too keep our distance from him, refusing to greet him or speak to him when someone says he has arrived—until, perhaps, he should call us each by name. Though Jesus himself seems greatly disturbed in spirit at both the deaths we have experienced and the doubts that grip us—he too is deeply agitated at the realities of death—somewhere beneath and in spite of all we continue to believe that he will speak the life-giving word at last (John 11:22-44).

For that word we wait, much as Mary and Martha did on that day in Bethany, though neither they nor we can imagine what might happen when Jesus speaks whatever word he finally says. And till then we pray, repeating the same words, believing what we have been taught, and not believing it at all. Lord, help our unbelief.

But beneath all of the doubting and waiting there is longing. Even beneath our fears and anger we long to be God's people, the people, one people.

———— • ————

In Philadelphia, as we prepared to board the plane for Tel Aviv, I sent a quick e-mail to my church members: "May it be not only that we go to Jerusalem, but that the new Jerusalem comes to us, out of heaven, as it were, to redeem the earth and all that is within it" (see Rev. 21:1; Ps. 24:1).

Summary

Our baptism unites us with people of all times and places in the great family of God. We are not isolated individuals on a solitary spiritual quest. Rather, in our words, stories, and experiences we find our identity with and among others in the one, holy, catholic church.

Questions for Reflection

1. Where have you seen evidence that you are not alone in your faith journey?
2. Where have you seen "deep" cooperation among churches that suggested to you a church beyond your congregation?

4

THE PLACES OF PRAYER

*Someone asked Abba Anthony, "What must one do in order
to please God?" The old man replied, "Pay attention to what I tell you:
whoever you may be, always have God before your eyes;
whatever you do, do it according to the testimony of the
holy Scriptures; in whatever place you live, do not easily leave it.
Keep these three precepts and you will be saved."*

ABBA ANTHONY

When I traveled to the Holy Land I found myself stunned by the rugged topography of the place. I had seen pictures, but two-dimensional interest gave way to three-dimensional wonder—and perhaps not only three. There was height. There was depth. There was width. And there was *spirit*.

I gawked, I shook my head, I took a thousand pictures of *rocks*, of dust, of the places, the particularities of *Israel*. *This* is where Jesus walked and talked, and before him all the heroes (and villains!) of our faith trekked here. What startled me most were the stark contrasts all around our group.

The Galilee was relatively, *relatively* green; but in the south, in Judea and the "disputed territories" of the West Bank, there was almost no green at all, except for the fabulous symmetrical rows of date palm trees that, here and there, form oases. Otherwise, it was all rocks and crags, mountains that erupted almost straight up out of the ground.

What might it mean, I wondered, *to realize the Ten Commandments were given in such a context, or that the children of Israel spent eras in such an environment, between Egypt and the land of promise?* Jesus himself went into this very wilderness to be tested and tempted, to determine what sort of messiah God would have him be.

What might such *surfaces* tell us about the kind of people we are to be? How might these broken precincts of our spiritual homeland themselves call us back from the "broad" paths down which our preaching and teaching wander, destructively awry?

Many preachers and teachers soften the crags and make the gospel "greener" than it is, preach "smooth" things. There is a ruggedness to the gospel that many in this culture try to round off.

If God promises one day to level the grounds and straighten the crooked, that day is not yet nor that job finally ours. Till then both the deep abyss (the Dead Sea) and the great high peaks (Sinai, Nebo, Horeb, Hermon) will remain, and all manner of terrain in between. These holy grounds characterize not only our faith's land of origin but also our own journeys of faith.

And what might any of that say about prayer? The ways and sorts of prayers we might pray now?

Caves here and there formed natural "cells," places of solitude where monks, saints, and holy men and women through the ages entered to purify themselves from the corruptions of the world, purging their souls by prayers and fasting. They would emerge now and then from their cells, join their brothers and sisters for meals, communal prayers, and ritual baths. Solitude founded the community; community empowered the solitude.

The Life of Cells

Interesting word: *cell.* One thinks of biology, those small units of protoplasm, the arena for complex chemical reactions that produce life. All living organisms have cells, one or many, as does the church. We are the body of Christ, and if in the early days the church was so small, so embryonic, that Paul could say each person was a member of it, these days, perhaps, we might see ourselves as cells in it. That does not diminish our role or value: gifts, graces, aptitudes are in each cell's DNA; but, of course, disease begins there too.

Biology is the least of it. We think of jail, of prison. Some are in literal cells, physically incarcerated because of crimes they have committed. Many serve hard time in prisons of their own making or keeping because of shame, guilt, fear, tragedy—or who knows all else why. Some cells connote only isolation.

I first learned the word *cell* from my dad, an electrical engineer, who taught me a little about batteries and the cells where electricity was channeled, or produced, and stored for later use.

And *cell* also means the smallest organizational unit of any group, movement, or organization.

What might it mean for us to go into or come out of our cells? To see even our solitude as a part of greater community? To see both ourselves and our churches as living cells? Or our prayers as attentive residence in and to the wilderness?

Several years ago Kathleen Norris wrote a book called *Dakota: A Spiritual Geography*.[1] In an exercise that would have pleased Abba Anthony—and also Saint Benedict, with whose spiritual heirs she was praying at the time—Ms. Norris took pains to tie not only prayers and praying but a deeper spirituality to the particularity of place. I read the book long ago, but I still think about that very spiritual practice: letting *place*—this place, this time, this circumstance—give shape to our prayers.

On the one hand, we do that all the time: pray about whatever it is that occupies us at the moment. But often those prayers are superficial, momentary, as isolated and isolating as jail. At least mine are.

I have prayed many days the way I used to play pinball: grabbing the sides of my life as I would the machine's, shooting the silver ball of my prayers up and around to make it drop among the bumpers and buzzers of the daily maze. Sometimes the ball careens a bit, bounces wildly off the edges of these concerns or those, back and forth, side-to-side, *ching! ching! ching!* I watch, push and nudge and muscle, work to make this turn count for something. But lots of times the ball rolls heavily and rapidly back toward me—whatever prayers I pray touch nothing at all but find the quick and empty path, *thunk*, into the dark hole that opens rather near my heart.

When I see that happening I push the buttons frantically, rock back and forth, try to keep the ball in play; but it finds the space between the flippers and disappears—just disappears. Almost as soon as I have started I am done again. My prayers return to me void and empty. Tilt.

Tilting, isolated, superficial, and frustrated self-absorbed prayers. Trying to score a few points to feel better about myself.

That kind of particularity is not what Abba Anthony or Saint Benedict or Ms. Norris is suggesting. Nor those who entered the wilderness to pray, away from the distractions of city and culture—though in the wilderness, they found they had distractions enough and greater on the inside, in heart and mind.

No, each in his or her own way and word, along with untold other writers and saints and monks by teaching and example, is calling us to a deeper excavation, beneath the often dry surface of things, for the rich aquifer of grace, the life-giving water that is somewhere below the dust and boulders. And should we find ourselves in the midst of ruins, there may yet be treasure. And refreshment. Indeed, our prayers and devotions are at best a kind of spiritual archaeology and all of us are together on a dig.

Rains in the Wilderness

Sudden rains come in the wildernesses of Israel, such hard rains as to produce dangerous slides and flash floods. But the torrential rains are sporadic, often momentary, and so in the ruins of every settlement, every town or palace, are great cisterns. We saw many in most every place, built here and there to catch the occasional meteorological blessing. Cisterns testify that long stretches of no rain at all—even in the rainy season—and long dry seasons characterize life in the desert.

Arid stretches also characterize our experience of God's presence and absence. Wherever we find ourselves, in whatever wilderness or camp, there are long dry seasons when it seems God is so very absent, when our spirits are so very dry and barren. But unexpectedly, suddenly, and often with overwhelming effect—there is more than we can absorb in a moment—refreshing comes and what we wouldn't give to have spiritual cisterns to catch and hold the blessing in reserve, cisterns to draw from when the dryness leaves us parched.

Or do we have them already? Are not the Font and the Table spiritual cisterns? Our clusters and classes, our Bible studies and prayer groups, even the long tradition of the church, the many prayers and spiritual disciplines bequeathed to us as gifts—are these not great repositories of refreshing, of faith and guidance like pools in the desert (Ps. 84:6-7), aquifers in the arid seasons? When we pray the prayers, observe the Hours, we find that we enter our cells and are the cells. We are in the body, and the body is in us, spanning time and space, joined with others who have believed and prayed, lived and died, with the hopes and prayers of God's people on their lips and in their hearts.

When we consider the *places* of prayer, we might well think only architecturally or geographically. We know of places where time, tradition, and the unceasing prayers of the people have created a cell, where even thick rock, natural or graven, forms a "thin place," a liminal space where heaven and earth may touch. In these places we glimpse past finitude and isolation into the life and future and family of God. We go to these places knowing that we are in position: that God may meet us as God has met so many others before. We may discover other places where real prayer takes hold of us. Indeed, the whole world is God's temple.

But cells can work the other way too. Cells can erect barriers and thicken walls.

Cell Phones I Have Known

I am no Luddite. Technology is a good thing; it can be a well of connectivity. But not always. Certain kinds of conversation at certain times distract and disrupt the task at hand, the *local* interactions that are part and parcel of any intimacy, physical or spiritual.

The daughter's phone started ringing during her mother's funeral! I was presiding at the service, looked from the pulpit to see her scrambling with her purse, trying to silence it. At once I felt both pity and anger, embarrassment for her and incredulity and rage at whoever on earth might be calling her at that time. Anyone who knew her at all knew she was distraught, was burying the mother with whom she had "issues," a strange and strained relationship; had herself attempted suicide some months before with some of those very issues as the trigger.

And maybe that was it. I began to calm. Maybe the one calling was a friend who could not be there, wanting to check on her quickly, as soon as the friend thought the service to be over, to see if she made it through all right. In fact, the service had run long—there were many words of witness. The friend may have calculated the daughter was out of the sanctuary, perhaps on the way to the cemetery. Maybe what we heard was the ring of sensitivity.

Still.

And for me it was the third such experience over a short course of days, all of them pointing to the same truth: our *devices*, while promising greater connection with those we know and love (and even with strangers), do nothing so much as disconnect us, distance us, distract us, and increase rather than alleviate the isolation and loneliness many of us feel. Yes, of course, they can web us together— just as *gossip* has the power to keep people connected. But if good gossip often morphs into dark and isolating speech, so too does communication through our phones and computers and such. The well is easily poisoned.

A few years ago at an annual meeting of the clergy in our area, our leaders urged us to form "Covenant Peer Groups," small cells of prayer and support. I circled up with seven others. We met biweekly, prayed and conversed, and soon found that we depended on our time together.

One of our meetings took place near the Feast of Saint Benedict. That seemed appropriate: after all, what we were doing felt a little bit monastic. But then one of our friends pulled out his cell phone to check for messages.

I was instantly furious, overreacting, due to a similar interruption a few evenings prior. My wife was leaving town for several days and we had arranged, with difficulty, to meet for dinner. We had been at the restaurant for maybe fifteen minutes when *her* cell phone buzzed and she, reaching for it, said perfunctorily, "Do you mind if I take this call?"

"No," I lied, but she was already gone, never really returned to our table, meal, or conversation. Her flight had already departed.

I have no doubt the issue was pressing. That said, I also received the unmistakable message as to who and what were more important to her in that moment. Yes, I lied, and was therefore complicit, but I am also certain that our little intimacy, such as it was, would have dissipated just as surely with the truth.

"Pay attention to *me*!" is what I wanted to say at the restaurant and in the meeting. What I wanted to say at the funeral was "Pay attention to *this*! To this place. This thing we are doing. This holy conversation. This prayer."

And I did manage, on the spot, to say something like that to my peer group friend. I managed, later, to say it also to my wife, with the honest confession that I knew I had treated her the same way on countless occasions.

I never said it to the daughter at all.

The paradox is that tending to the local, the here and now—this conversation, this prayer, this place—is what unites us to the wider fellowship. When we eschew the here and now we lose "the present company" and threaten future intimacies.

We see this threat all the time: folks in a restaurant with their cell phones talking to people other than those at the table with them. We do it all the time: put people on hold while we take another call. We experience it all the time, being shuttled by device and distraction to somebody's subroutine. In any case the message is always the same: whoever that might be, they need my attention more than you do; whatever this call might concern, it is more important than the present conversation; whoever or whatever is "out there" or "coming in" is more interesting than this or you or now.

Through my years as a pastor I have been accused more than a few times—and often rightly—of giving most of my best attentions and energies to others, whether parishioners or strangers rather than to those closest to me. My wife and children have said it over and over: "*We* need you here! We need you *here!*" In the past, such discussions and disagreements seemed relational and proportional, mostly concerned with *my* clock or calendar (and sometimes consciousness). Of late, though, the issue has gone viral and presents itself as increasingly spiritual, theological in fact.

A few weeks before any of these unpleasant moments, a different group of ministers had gathered in the basilica at Belmont Abbey for both Word and Table and, later, prayer with the monks. In between, Abbot Placid, the abbey's prior, joined our group after worship and prayer to teach us that for all the bewildering variety of religious orders in Roman Catholic life, each falls into one or the other of two basic categories: apostolic or monastic. The former, such as the Jesuits, move out into the world to fulfill their vocation. The latter, such as the Benedictines, pledge themselves to one place and, in effect, to one conversation: prayer.

If the apostolic orders teach us that every hearth is an altar, every place a cell, every service a kind of prayer, the monastic orders teach us that there are specific places to pray and specific prayers to be prayed. Neither is complete without the other, but the latter is harder for us in this culture. Even the "religious," those vowed to a life of prayer in a particular context, can find themselves moving about frenetically in the world, frantically fashioning their own peculiar ministries with their own discrete techniques.

But *one* place and *one* conversation. This place. These prayers. It is a fetching notion and rooted in traditions older than Benedict.

The actual places may change, but deep prayer is always tied to context. And for some, the contexts of their praying do not change at all. The most countercultural form of spiritual practice available to us may indeed be the kinds of prayers, worship, and witness that are suffused with the *local*. If not monastic exactly, such a perspective is monastic practically: pledging self to this place and this conversation, whichever place and conversation that happens to be, whether in a meeting or at dinner, in prayer or while counseling, whether studying or writing. "A monastery without walls," is the way Eugene

Peterson describes it,[2] describing also the attitude I am trying to cultivate in my own ministry. I am trying to live my life and fulfill my own vocation by the Benedictine premise: paying attention to this, to what is before me here and now.

Kallistos Ware says that the beginning and end of this kind of praying, called *physiki*, is precisely this: to cultivate the awareness that any moment, any place or person, "is holy, each is in its own way unrepeatable and so of infinite value, [that] each can serve as a window into eternity."[3] This church—not my next church or my former one; not even *the* church, so much as *this* church—and these people, one conversation at the time.

That effort seems to me not only monastic in some sense but also incarnational: bringing myself into relationship not just proximity; into intimacy and avoiding as best I can the incessant, disembodied, Gnostic summons *elsewhere*. The more distracting summons of tweeting, texting, and Facebook seem to be "emanations" of what a young colleague calls the "whole other world" of cyberspace. Incarnation demands that when disembodied distractions come, as they inevitably do—whether passions, thoughts, or tweets—I pray myself back to the moment in order to stay present, attentive, attuned not to the voices but to the Voice. Not to the next place but to *this* place.

One Place, One Conversation

On Palm and Passion Sunday, as we read the Gospel of Luke's account of Holy Week's beginnings, I could not help but notice how "noisy" the text is: how often "voices" and "shouts" accompanied Jesus and how quiet he seems to have been in turn. He instructs the disciples about the donkey; he responds to the Pharisees. Otherwise, he is silent, resolute—as if voices, whether the disciples' or the crowd's, will not distract him. His attention to the heavenly Voice and purpose centers him.

Incarnation, monasticism: one place and one conversation. The apostolic orders are incarnational too, and daily we ourselves are likewise summoned into the wider world, carrying the message and effecting the ministry of reconciliation. That said, many times those of us who are ambassadors of reconciliation actually work against this ministry, not least by separating ourselves from the people closest at hand in pursuit of distractions.

Urban Holmes suggested our distraction comes from the lack of a "center." This "center" is the primary place for prayer, portable and abiding, and crucial for real ministry. He tells of a moment, early in his first pastoral assignment, when "a constant stream of indigents came through. One came into my office and wanted to tell me his story. I sat as if to listen but was deeply troubled inside over some issue now long forgotten. I remember I was fiddling with a pencil. The man stopped his story, looked at me and said, 'Young Father, the least you can do is listen.'"4

Paying attention; not checking out; leaving messages and e-mail till later (what is voice mail *for* after all?); leaving the phone in the car when we enter a restaurant to eat; taking that damned thing out of our ears. These little spiritual practices might begin to incarnate a prophetic and pastoral critique of this noisy, disembodied age, an age in which ministers have been lampooned as, in Stanley Hauerwas's words, "quivering mass[es] of availability."5 The irony, of course, as C. S. Lewis and others have observed, is that such availability and busyness is, contrary to appearances, a form of *acedia*, the restlessness that is one of the dragon's heads!

What if we determined not to be always available to everyone but, as a way of doing the "least we can," which might also be at times the most we can: listening, being engaged, being both present and truly available to those in our charge? Such countercultural practices might be the new chastity!

Abbot Placid reminded the pastors in the group that Benedict greatly valued hospitality. His Rule (#53) includes this injunction: "Let all guests who arrive be treated as Christ, for he is going to say, 'I came as a guest and you received me' (Matt. 25:35). And to all let honor be shown." I would add, "especially to those right in front of me."

While it could be argued, I suppose, that answering the phone is itself a form of hospitality, of receiving a guest, I find myself thinking of Cleopas and his friend in Emmaus. The One at table with them is Jesus, but they do not recognize him. As Jesus takes the bread,

THE PLACES of PRAYER

prepares to bless, break, and give it to them, Cleopas interrupts: "Do you mind if I take this call?"

One Place for All People: The Temple

In 1 Kings 8, when Solomon dedicates the Temple in Jerusalem, we read in terms of prayer and doxology, an affirmation of God's faithfulness and majesty, of God's promise of provision. The doxology and the dedication and especially Solomon's petitions are rooted in the promises God made to Solomon's father, David. Solomon is simply, if powerfully, calling on God to keep God's promises—to make good what God has already said.

The prayer in 1 Kings 8 forms an interesting couplet with the covenant renewal text found in Joshua 24, where Joshua calls the people of God to pledge and promise their fealty to God and then to live according to that pledge and promise. Their pledge is rooted in God's past provision—the deliverance from Egypt and the "protect[ion] along all the way that we went" (Josh. 24:17)—but that memory is to be worked out in the present and the future. Memory is a huge part of both faithfulness and hope.

I have heard it said that while memory and hope are crucial to faith, hope is more crucial. That may be so. But in terms of liturgy, in terms of pledge—as regards the "places" of our prayers—memory is the more crucial. And when people forget past deliverance, along with the stories and prayers that tell and accompany that deliverance, they are likely to lose both faith and hope, their present and future identity along with their history.

Joshua calls the people to remember and act. He leads them in a liturgical interrogation that calls for communal affirmation: All that the Lord has said, we will do. Similarly, Solomon calls on God to remember and make pledge to the people, to answer Solomon's liturgical prayer, and not only for the sake of Israel and David.

The petition Solomon prays for strangers always moves me. He asks God to show his guests hospitality: "When a foreigner, who is not of your people Israel, comes from a distant land because of your name—for they shall hear of your great name, your mighty hand,

and your outstretched arm . . ." (1 Kings 8:41-42). In short, God's faithfulness will be evident in all the earth by means of the testimony of those who have seen God's greatness; and those "first believers" who trust the testimony will come to God, to this land and this place.

And when they do, Solomon asks God to hear the prayers of those who come, whoever they might be, "and [to] do according to all that the foreigner calls to you, so that all the peoples of the earth may know your name and fear you" (1 Kings 8:43). Not all will hear, and not all who hear will come; but if God remains faithful to answer the prayers of the strangers, all will eventually know and revere the God of Israel, "as do [the people of] Israel" (v. 43).

"When a foreigner comes" is a phrase worth pondering. . . . Solomon is praying not only for those who already believe in and are covenanted to the God of Israel, but those who will come to believe, and believing, will come to pray at the Temple. Some will come physically. Some will point their hearts, aim their prayer, toward Zion. He is praying for all who by faith and hope and prayer will be united across time and language and geography and politics, because God will keep the divine "eyes . . . open night and day toward this house (I Kings 8:29). Much as the writer of Ephesians says that Christians are but the first to set their hope on Christ (Eph. 1:12), Solomon anticipates a great unity that will come by means of prayer itself.

Solomon's prayer is a powerful one. God answers Solomon in the next chapter. And if the answer comes to Solomon alone (1 Kings 9:1-3), the answer is for all people: God affirms that the covenant to David will be continued in Solomon's reign and beyond.

During the prayer "when the priests came out of the holy place, a cloud filled the house of the LORD, so that the priests could not *stand* to minister because of the cloud" (1 Kings 8:10-11, emphasis added). The cloud of God's presence, the cloud of unknowing, the cloud of un-ministering. If we in our culture often talk about illumination as the goal of spirituality and prayer, the Eastern traditions and this text remind us that sometimes God's presence blinds and confuses, overwhelms, and, as it were, unhorses us.

That is an interesting word too: *unhorse.* I was just trying to find a synonym for "overwhelm," but the image came to mind of God's powerful presence as an unsettling judgment and grace. Pharaoh's troops were unhorsed by God's power at the sea, their inability to stand a sign both of God's judgment and of God's gracious deliverance of Israel. Our inability to "stand to minister" is likewise a sign of God's judgment and pardon, God's presence and grace.

At times we stand too easily, keep on our feet too comfortably—and that is a sign of self-reliance and distance from God. We seldom take to our knees; though sometimes we are knocked, unhorsed, from our high horses. On our knees—that is the place of prayer.

———•———

I traveled to the Holy Land with friends, confident that Solomon's prayer from long ago was answered and is still being answered. I, a foreigner, went there because I had heard of God's great name, God's mighty hand and outstretched arm—an arm outstretched enough to embrace this stranger with loving hospitality. I pray that as I pray, God's eyes and ears will keep open day and night to hear and answer my call. I remember, hope, and trust that my prayers in that place were worthy of the ones prayed before them, the prayers of Solomon and others, and that God has mercy and hears *my* prayers, our prayers.

I came as a stranger to the place where Solomon prayed for me. And so I pray for those who come to the church, any church—but especially my church and find it as strange a "land" as Israel was for me. I pray that when people come, God will hear them. And I believe God will and does.

I also pray that I will be granted to pray with them, that our family can become their family, our home their home. That the prayers of our congregation will be their prayers, and our worship their praise.

Summary

As is true of faith, the Christian experience of prayer begins with the concrete and particular: a time, a place, a people and a history. Prayer is a "universalizing" spiritual discipline; its arc is expansive and inclusive, drawing all within its span. But the genesis of such praying is tied *first* to specifics. Prayer, therefore, is a *contextual,* not an ethereal, exercise.

Questions for Reflection

1. How does your particular place and context help you universalize your prayers?
2. How do you see yourself, your class, your church, your denomination—and each of these in this present time or moment—as a cell or a place of prayer?

5

THE TIMES OF PRAYER

From their earliest moments, the three monotheistic faiths of
Abraham—Judaism, Christianity, and Islam—have all shared
certain assumptions about, and disciplines of, religious and spiritual
formation. All three appoint one day each week as sacred unto God.
All three require tithing. Each encourages spiritual pilgrimage.
All three govern themselves according to the rhythms of a liturgical year;
and each teaches the use of fasting at appointed seasons . . .
[and] all three have, from their very inception, assumed the practice
of fixed-hour prayer as part and parcel of the observant life. . . .
Because the hours of prayer were fixed or set, one could stop wherever
one was, be it alone or in company, and offer the appointed words of
praise and thanksgiving, knowing thereby that one was part of the
whole company of believers worshiping together across geography and
circumstance before the throne of God.

PHYLLIS TICKLE

In monastic tradition, the day is sectioned, intersected, by prayers:
Lauds, Prime, Terce, Sext, None, Vespers, Compline, and Matins.
These are the canonical Hours. To observe them is to keep the Divine
Office. Monks come out of their cells to pray together, to form and
reform their communities. Breviaries and prayer books help, for they
are the basic script.

There are various sequences in the many traditions, sometimes ending in the cool of the evening or in the cold just before midnight; sometimes beginning with the dusky dawn of a new Jewish day or the deep darkness of the third-hour *ante meridiem*—very early in the morning, as when the women went to the tomb. The spiritual day, the devotional day, dances to the seven-beat rhythm of prayer. Prayers do too, though sometimes they shuffle: this daily waltz with the Hours can be a slow, monotonous step, and the ones who keep at it sometimes look like those poor folk in the twenties and thirties who entered dance marathons and at the end had to lean on each other just to keep going, to stay on their feet. Those who pray the Hours, likewise.

But sometimes there comes joy, pure joy, a sensation on the other side of the work and monotony. Annie Dillard has written that "at its best, the sensation of writing is that of any unmerited grace. It is handed to you, but only if you look for it. You search, you break your heart, your back, your brain and then—and only then—it is handed to you. From the corner of your eye you see motion. Something is moving through the air and headed your way."[1]

Prayer too can be like that. We show up, we settle down, we open the books and open our mouths. Words come out and something comes in, some sense, some grace, some joy, some realization that these same words, prayed over time, are given to us to pray in our time, because the Hours' words are our words. We pray the same prayers that have in all times and places been prayed by those who worship the God of Abraham, the Father of our Lord Jesus Christ, the King of the universe, blessed be he. We pray and they prayed, and in the praying there is no longer they and we, divided by time and geography—but only "we" period. The communion of the saints. The company of pray-ers.

There comes a thrill now and then, an unmerited joy like grace on the other side of the work, on the other side of the liturgy, like rain in the desert to settle and soften the dust and furrows of our hearts, to moisten our dry spirits.

Each Hour has a theme, a *key* if you will—though there is variation even here and the theme is not always explicit. All the Hours' music is point and counterpoint, an interweaving of praise and repentance.

Lauds, prayed under the first rays of sunrise: praise for the morning, the gift of renewal. **Prime**, just after Lauds: repentance at the hour Jesus appeared before Pilate, the reality of sin clearly illumined. **Terce**, at 9 a.m.: praise again at the hour when the Holy Spirit was given in power on Pentecost. **Sext**, at noon: repentance at the hour of Jesus' crucifixion. **None**, at 3 p.m.: deep contrition at the hour of Jesus' death. **Vespers**, and with Lauds the most ancient of Christian "hours," at sunset: according to the Jewish calendar the beginning of a new day and the re-creation of the world. **Compline**, when before bedtime we ponder our own deaths, trusting our deaths and our lives into the hands of God. **Matins**, sometimes called **Vigils**, the latest or the earliest prayers, and not always observed, but prayers to fill the dark till light and Lauds arrive.

Some of the services are longer: Matins, Vigils. Most are rather short, the breviary somewhat brief: fifteen minutes or so. Fifteen minutes, seven times a day. But that is almost two hours of communal prayer, not counting the other ways and times monks and nuns and others pray.

Some traditions divide the week too, each day having its own theme or key. The purpose, the rationale, the discipline is the "holying" of time: setting apart hours and days for God's purposes, for God's praise, for our faith and faithfulness.

Now and then I pray with a group of monks. Entering the cool chancel of their basilica, I take a seat near them but not among them: at a respectful distance, you might call it. They enter, robed, and cowled some of them, in ones and twos. They genuflect to the altar and take their assigned seats.

The choir stall where the monks sit is divided, flanking the area between the altar and the abbot's chair at the very front. For several minutes there is silence—to allow the brothers and their guests to arrive and also to allow space and time for monks to center themselves, to reassemble themselves as a group, to pray for prayer's sweet return. In fact, there is a sweetness—a fragrance—in the room: the slate floor, the worn pews, the woolen cowls, a slight mustiness from the missals.

Soon the monks begin: call back and forth to one another across the distance. It is the ordinary form of their praying, but it strikes my ear as more than tradition. It seems as if the monks are reminding one another what, if they prayed alone, they might forget to pray; if indeed alone, they prayed at all.

There are several psalms. A reading. Silence in between. Soon, they rise, offer corporate intercession and benediction "for our absent brothers." They close the prayer books, file out, bow to the altar in turn, then bow again to one another, their eyes averted. The coolness, the silence, the smells linger.

Three times a day, sometimes more, monks gather to pray in such a way. They order their lives by prayer. Prayer intersects their work, and their work feeds their prayers. Day by day, week by week, month by month, and year by year for a lifetime. It is a holy, forming work, and often shames my sputtering, sporadic orisons.

Ora et labora—prayer and work. That is the regimen of a monk's life. Prayer and work. Working and praying. Working *at* praying: that too. Prayer is hard work, a hard thing, maybe the hardest thing, a fight to the last breath one desert father said.[2] Thomas Mann, author of *Death in Venice*, once said that an author is one for whom writing is more difficult than it is for others. Counterintuitive but exactly right.

So maybe Christians are those for whom prayer is more difficult than it is for others—but who keep praying nonetheless, who struggle to the last to speak and to listen, who know that, as Saint Theophan the Recluse said, "Prayer is the test of everything. . . . If prayer is right, everything is right."[3] We confess that we have not got it right yet, and so we keep at it.

Annie Dillard tells of a well-known writer who "got collared" by a university student. The student asked, "Do you think I could be a writer?" The writer thought for a moment and said, "I don't know. Do you like sentences?" The writer, she says, "could see the student's amazement. Sentences? Do I like sentences? I am twenty years old and do I like sentences? If he had liked sentences, of course, he could begin, like a joyful painter I knew. I asked him how he came to be a painter. He said, 'I liked the smell of the paint.'"[4]

Do I like to pray? I am sixty years old, almost; do I like to pray? Do I like the smell of prayer?

Yes. I do. But it is hard work. Hard to begin, hard to maintain, and sometimes, by grace, hard to stop once we have started. So how to start?

Not alone, I think. Or not always. And especially not at first. We need help. We need brothers and sisters. We need the apostles, the prophets, the martyrs, our elders and betters in the faith. We need the tradition and friends to help us . . . the Psalms and the "company of Jesus," as Eugene Peterson calls the church.[5]

We need help to do it right.

Our Life in Jesus' Life

The temporal cycle. The Christian year. The liturgy of the seasons. The year is divided too, like the day. The seasons tell the story of Jesus' life: Advent. Christmas. Epiphany. Lent. Triduum. Easter. Pentecost.

Advent is Mary's last month, the last gestures of gestation and the first pangs of birth, God's redemption on its way but not yet with us. Christmas is Jesus' first days, God with us, King of the Jews, Emmanuel. Epiphany is the dawn of God's rule for all the world: this One, born King of the Jews, is Savior of all, and the coming of the magi proves it. Lent: the powers that be will resist the kingdom to come and for Jesus to be the Savior of all, he will suffer at the hands of a few. Triduum: the powers of darkness overwhelm the light, but they will not overcome the light: the Cross is the worst we can do to God or to ourselves, but darkness will be trumped by a new day, early on the first morning of the eighth comes new life, God's new creation. Easter: God refuses to let sinful humanity's "no" be the last word. The Resurrection is God's defiant "yes *anyway*." Pentecost: Jesus sends the Holy Spirit in power to make good the promise that "you shall be my witnesses" (Acts 1:8, RSV). The promise is a command, the command a promise, and the Holy Spirit inspires both.

Christians tell the time and tell the times by this calendar, and we have for long ages. At first the rationale was pedagogical: most Christians were illiterate; the worship of the church iterated and reiterated the life of Jesus. The various lectionaries were developed to assist the church in its narrations of the Savior's life.

Now the rationale is more spiritual: we see in the temporal cycle the story of Jesus' life, and in that way we illumine our own lives' journeys.[6] At least that is the goal.

Advent: not only Mary's last month but Israel's time in the wilderness, awaiting the Promised Land; and we ourselves in the wilderness, something of God's will and purpose conceived and gestating within us, but when will it come? **Christmas:** Jesus says that whoever does the will of God is his brother, his sister, his *mother* (Mark 3:35), all of us *theotokoi*,[7] birthing Jesus into this godless world by our own praise and obedience.

Epiphany: the particularity of our gospel makes it universal in scope, so that we no longer regard anyone from a human (read: cultural) point of view (2 Cor. 5:16), but all as part of God's new creation. **Lent:** we engage, incarnate, embody God's redemption in the world, faithful to our vows even at cost to ourselves (Ps. 15:4), denying ourselves in order to take up a cross and follow Jesus. **Triduum:** the darkness often overwhelms us, and we are given to sadness and grief. **Easter:** weeping tarries for the Triduum, but joy comes in the early morning. We are heirs to the new life breaking loose in the world. **Pentecost:** we are ambassadors of Christ, God appealing to the world through us. We have the ministry and the message of reconciliation—not one without the other—and are empowered agents of God's kingdom, of Christ's peace in the world.

Our Death in Jesus' Life

At a funeral not long ago, I did something odd, though not everyone noticed, not at first: I left the purple paraments instead of switching them to white.

White is the usual color for funerals. Purple is the color for Lent, which is when this funeral took place, the forty-day remembrance of Jesus' suffering. Purple is the color of that increasingly sad season, those weeks in which we recall how Jesus was tempted in the wilderness, rejected by his own people, betrayed by his own disciples, arrested by his own religious authorities; then tried, whipped, and killed by foreign occupiers, political authorities. . . . It is a pretty color, this purple, but a sad color too.

Which is why, most times, even in the middle of Lent, we change the purple to white and gold, hang white and gold paraments because those are the colors of Easter, Easter Day, and Easter Season, the Great Fifty Days of Resurrection remembrance and proclamation. On and during Easter we proclaim that *death* is not the final word or the defining word: God's gift of new life is! God's life given in the face of death: that is what Jesus experienced and what Jesus promised and what, we believe, all the faithful enjoy on the other side of their suffering.

But we left the purple this one time. Why?

Partly because in the sanctuary stood a great wooden cross for our congregation's observance of Lent. A large purple cloth adorned it and at its base were symbols of the season: ashes, thirty silver coins, a rooster, a sponge, a sword and whip. Couldn't move all that. I thought to try, but then I remembered that the first time I ever met Barbara, the deceased, she sat in my office and asked me to do her funeral. Her lung cancer was already well-advanced. She knew she was going to die. And she needed someone to preside when the time came. A member of my church said she would do the introductions, and so they came to see me, together.

We sat and we talked; we discussed the service and we prayed. We laughed, and when she asked if I would, indeed, officiate, we cried. I was so *honored* for her to trust me in such a way.

Somewhere in there we talked about her uneven relationship with the church over the years—not with God or with Jesus and the Holy Spirit: that relationship was rock-solid—but it had been years since she was in a church or part of a church.

So I invited her to come be a part of our congregation, though even as I asked we knew it would not be for very long. "Let us gather around you," I said, "walk with you, hold you up in prayer. Let us be your spiritual family as you approach the dark gates of eternal life and light."

And she did. On December 16. During Advent, in other words, the four-week run-up to Christmas Day and the Christmas season. In those four Advent weeks we recall Israel's long wait for its Messiah; we remember Mary's last, uncomfortable month of pregnancy—and how, when the time came, she gave birth in a strange place in a strange town among strangers. In Advent we proclaim the joy that awaits us on the other side of painful reality, the Promised Land that awaits us on the other side of the wilderness, the reconciliations that await us on the other side of our many estrangements.

The color for Advent—like the color for Lent—is purple.

Barbara joined our church with the color of Advent all around her, suffering so much already, but in hopes I think that after her own last uncomfortable months, here, in this strange place, a place she had never been, among strangers who would soon be friends—that in the midst of new friends and spiritual family, when her time came, she would be delivered of her pain and find joy.

You could see something of her joy, of her hope, something of her faith in her "new member picture" that remained on the board in the hall: her smile was bright to the last, even the last time I saw her, just a couple of days before she died. I took her fevered hand and prayed with her one last time. Behind her in the picture was our Table, draped in purple, the color of Advent, the color of suffering hope.

Only a few months later she left our congregation with purple, the color of Lent, all around: the color of hopeful suffering. She had suffered, but with the sure and certain hope that the pain is not greater than the release, that death is not stronger than resurrection, that the sufferings of this present time are not worthy to be compared with the glory that is to be revealed to us (Rom. 8:18).

Advent gives way to Christmas and Lent to Easter. Suffering gives way to victory and lamentation to song. Purple may be the color of our lives on this side of the river, but every funeral day becomes the day of the Lord, and all will be white, and all will be white, and all will be whiter than snow.

Barbara came to us in Advent; she left us in Lent. And it was such an *honor* for her to trust our church in such a way. And a blessing for her too as loneliness gave way to community: she did not walk that path alone, not completely. As she approached the dark gates to eternal light and life she had us with her, and then on the other side of them, on that far shore in a brighter light, a greater church that without ceasing sings praise to the Lamb.

Times and Tallow

Gestures and liturgy attend the seasons: Advent candles, the Twelve Days of Christmas, Easter vigils and sunrise services, giving up something for Lent.

The third Sunday of Advent is Gaudete Sunday, but the meaning of the day is as obscure and unpronounceable as its name. In the earliest days of its observance, Advent was a penitential season, characterized by fasting and mortification: the appropriate postures to lament the necessity of Christ's coming to die. The pastoral benefit was that by taking things away from themselves, Christians might create in themselves space into which holiness might be born. As someone fashioned the manger in Bethlehem that Jesus might be laid there, we fashion emptiness in hopes God might fill it with our Lord.

The other idea is this: What can you give God, after all? God *has* everything. Perhaps the only way to give anything to God is by taking something away from ourselves. The old word for such a gift given to God is *mortification*. Sadly, while God does not give us rocks when we ask for bread, God asks for so little of us and we give even less.

Urban T. Holmes writes about mortification in connection with Lent:

> *Mortification is the intentional denial of legitimate pleasures in the spirit of Christian poverty that one might become more human. In my tradition Lent has long been considered a time for mortification, although one would not use such a "medieval" word. We gave up eating desserts, going to movies, or telling dirty jokes, all of which in the face of world problems seemed rather trivial. Once rendered silly, we dismissed the idea of "giving up"*

*and talked of "taking on." What we failed to understand was
that a life incapable of significant sacrifice is also incapable of
courageous action.*[8]

I have long pondered that particular quotation, finding it increasingly significant as both challenge and summons.

I grew up as a Southern Baptist, went to a denominational college and a once-fine seminary, but came very nearly to the end of my Baptist days knowing nothing of the Hours, the Christian seasons, nor of mortification, of fasting.

I do not blame my heritage, for I am sure there was plenty of opportunity for me to experience a wider expression of faith and worship, but I was in seminary before I ever recall hearing the word *Advent* and had no idea then or for a long while what it meant. Nor did I ask, in case others did. I wonder why I didn't look it up?

I still remember the day, in our weekly doctoral colloquium, when one of our colleagues came in dressed in dark clothing with an ash smudge on her head—and I was not alone in expressing confusion as to what it might mean. All that to say, I did not grow up with Advent wreaths or Ash Wednesday observances, much less with any emphasis on the traditional spiritual disciplines. And if I had heard of them, I am sure—son of the revivals as I was—I would have lumped all of that "stuff" together: religion, outward forms, ceremony, ignorance, sin. Here and there, though, now and then, I gradually began to sense the beauty and power of ritualized and corporate recollection—that the faith was not only *personal* but was a gift to the community and to members of it.

One December I went to a "formal" Baptist church near the seminary and saw my first Advent wreath. The candle lighting was simple but elegant, with scripture, a brief narration of its meaning, a choral response. A colleague of mine was aghast! The whole thing was *Catholic! Creedal!*

Maybe, but I found it appealing. Beautiful. Meaningful.

No church I served during that time would have countenanced either an Advent wreath or the liturgy that attended it, but I kept it in mind. Later, after many unexpected partings and pilgrimages, I landed in a United Methodist church where I began to feel right at home. The seasons, the disciplines, the narrative logic of the Christian year grounded me, gave me an identity and my worship a nerve. I had found an "old-time religion" that was, finally, almost old enough.

Later still, when I had heard the call to resume my ministry in a United Methodist context, I took a four-point "charge," four small churches united in paying one full-time pastor they shared among them. The first Sunday of the first Advent I served there, I walked into a small sanctuary to find an Advent wreath recently rescued, after some years, from the supply closet. The wreath had four white candles in a circle surrounding a large purple one in the center.

For decades now I have advocated the traditional arrangement— purple, purple, pink, purple, white. On account of Frederick Buechner, Urban Holmes, and my own commitment to the tradition, I have lobbied against the blue. But I may be in the mood for a change.

Specifically, I think the new arrangement should be three pinks and one purple. Could we agree to incorporate at least *one* week of mortification into the season? It is clear that Advent, December, the run-up to Christmas, is no longer about emptying space in preparation for the holy, either in ourselves or in our churches. Instead, we fill the days and weeks with every possible activity, consumption, acquisition. There is so much busyness and no sabbath, no self-denial. Maybe we could just take one Sunday and yes, I know, Sunday is not to be a fast day, but one *day*, a Sunday or otherwise, to mortify, to fast and pray and deny "legitimate pleasures in the spirit of Christian poverty that [we] might become more human" . . . or even more Christian?

There may be something to that.

Prayers and Places

There are special times for prayer, connected to our special places.

The Font: a place for prayer and a time for prayer, for the specific kind of prayer we call *examen*: remembering who we *really* are and are *really* called to be by recalling the baptism and prayers of Jesus. Luke's telling of the story of Jesus' baptism is quite pastoral, serene, even: Jesus, damp with his obedience, wet with his baptism, and praying. Praying!

And it is only when Jesus has been baptized and is praying that the heavens are opened and the Holy Spirit descends in bodily form as a dove. The dove, the Spirit, comes as a promise and pledge of God's presence for whatever Jesus will soon face in his ministry. We recall the text of Isaiah 43:

> *But now thus says the L*ORD*, he who created you, O Jacob,*
> *he who formed you, O Israel:*
> *Do not fear, for I have redeemed you;*
> *I have called you by name, you are mine.*
> *When you pass through the waters, I will be with you;*
> *and through the rivers, they shall not overwhelm you;*
> *when you walk through fire you shall not be burned,*
> *and the flame shall not consume you.* (Isa. 43:1-2)

The promise of accompaniment through water and river and flame and fire—that was crucial for Jesus, and for us. The difficulties are real, but so is the promised presence. Not protection but deliverance.

In recent years the church has done a good job of reclaiming baptism as the "fountain" of all ministry. We have acknowledged and affirmed the ministry of "all" the baptized—the water on our heads as commission and pledge. We have not done so good a job, I think, of reclaiming prayer as equal partner with baptism for the purposes of ministry. Maybe we think that goes without saying. But in fact it must be said: Prayer is essential for ministry. The Holy Spirit comes when we are both baptized and praying!

Note well: We do not believe in "private" baptisms. We believe baptism should take place in the context of worship, in the presence of the assembled, in the midst of praise and proclamation under the authority of scripture and tradition. We can work out the ministry of our baptism, incarnate our baptism, remember our baptism more or less privately; but baptism itself is a corporate act.

Likewise, we should believe that prayer too is first and foremost a matter of community, that it takes place in the context of worship, in company with the assembled, under the authority of scripture and tradition—in fact, formed by scripture and tradition. We will pray at other times in other ways too; privately, at Table, in the world. But prayer at its best is always a function of the faithful community. And even when we are praying alone, we are given prayers to pray that help us form identity across distance and time with the living and the dead and the as yet unborn: an unbroken praise, stretching back to the first songs of the morning stars and forward to the unending doxologies of the new Jerusalem. We simply take our place in the company of faith.

Yes, Jesus prays alone. In one way. But he is representative of Israel—the remnant, as it were. His prayers are the prayers of all God's people and will be portrayed as unceasing intercession. And as he prays with and for all God's people, the heavens themselves are opened and the Spirit descends as a dove, as gentle peace.

The Table: That is another special place and time.

The waitress hands me my check and a fortune cookie and with a thick accent says, "Thank you!" I slide out of the booth and walk past steaming buffet tables of shrimp and onions, pepper chicken, rice noodles, and sushi—the sushi table does not steam; it is chilled. I *love* the sushi.

I stand in line to pay, pay the same amount, most every day, because almost every day I eat the very same food at the very same place: the price of the buffet, no charge for water with no ice, but an extra dollar for the sushi chef's tip bowl.

Did I mention that I *love* the sushi? And the word *sushi*, by the way, does not refer to raw fish; it refers to the *rice* the fish is rolled in. And with the fish, most of which is cooked, by the way, and not raw, there is avocado and cucumber and pickled seaweed—which sounds odd and icky to our ears but is no odder, I would suggest, no ickier, than pickled eggs or pickled okra. Add a small dollop of hot wasabi, a bit of sweet ginger, the salt of the soy sauce—it is an oriental rainbow of flavors.

Yum.

I always pay the same price, because I pretty much always eat the same meal, and when I get to the cashier I always see the same thing—a bowl of peppermints. I always take a peppermint because, much as I love the sushi (and I did mention that, right? That I love the sushi?), I don't really want to spend the rest of the day with sushi on my breath.

Lots of other restaurants provide peppermints too: they come with the check if it is a nice place, or they are there on the counter as you check out.

But we don't serve peppermints at our church, even though we too are an "eating establishment." Which is to say, we serve Communion here and often: the same food, the same drink, at the same price. But no peppermints. Why might that be?

Because we want to leave here with Jesus on our breath. With "Jesus breath."

I think of that moment in Isaiah 6, when Isaiah saw God "high and lifted up" (v. 1, RSV). In the year that King Uzziah died, which was some seven hundred years before the time of Jesus, Isaiah heard the angels calling out "Holy, holy, holy" and when he heard them, Isaiah knew how *unholy* he was! *His* first word was confession: "I am a man of unclean lips, and I dwell in the midst of a people of unclean lips" (v. 5, RSV).

Isaiah was already a prophet, but he saw for himself the truth of what he had been preaching; and when he did, he saw the truth about himself, how ungodly he was—especially in his speech.

Just as we, if we had the vision, might see, hear, know that we live in a *world* of people of unclean lips, a culture as idolatrous and individualized as it can be, where often what we say cannot be distinguished from what anyone else says. With our lips we bless God but curse those made in God's image; with our lips we give service to God and disservice to God's servants and children. We sing praise to God, then judge, gossip, criticize. We too often, even in the church, speak the divisive and dividing and condescending word.

In Isaiah 6, an angel goes to the altar, takes a coal from the altar with tongs, and touches it to Isaiah's mouth. Isaiah will leave the Temple with altar fire and with God's words on his breath.

On Communion Sundays, Jesus gives us a piece of bread from the Table.

To purify our speech. And no peppermints at the back door either. Because we want to leave here with Jesus on our breath. With "Jesus breath."

Jesus breathed on the fearful, feckless disciples that first Easter night, that they might receive the Holy Spirit. When we take Communion we are reminded that Jesus would breathe on us his peace and forgiveness, and not for us alone, but that we might share that peace with others. And if we forgive the sins of any, they are forgiven (John 20:23). To that end Jesus gives us holy food, as much as coals from the Temple's altar, so that we will leave here with peace and forgiveness on our breath, so that *whoever* will be able to *smell* the difference in what we say.

Jesus breath. Jesus on our breath.

Every time we kneel to pray and every time we rise from prayer and go into the world to represent God in the world, we want Jesus on our breath.

Summary

Worship is unceasing praise of God. Still, worship has been historically ordered by the seasons of the temporal cycle or Christian year. In that way we give adequate attention to the whole story of Jesus' life and ministry, in light of Hebrew Scripture and the experience of the early church. In much the same way, the church calls its children to pray always and everywhere, indeed "without ceasing"; but the hours of prayer serve to shape and balance our praying, drawing our attention away from ourselves that we might ponder daily the greater will and purposes of God.

Questions for Reflection

1. Do you observe the Daily Office? If you do, what can you say about the difference it makes in your life, worship, vocation? If not, would you consider doing so, perhaps during Advent

or Lent? Can you imagine how it might change your prayers?

2. How have you experienced the sacraments to be moments when prayer and worship, time and eternity, the personal and the corporate intersect?

6

THE LANGUAGES OF PRAYER

"Corporate prayer," wrote Brother Roger [founder of Taizé] to his monks, "does not dispense us from personal prayer. The one sustains the other."... Personal prayer is not one of the things I struggle with. But if you flip over the line Brother Roger wrote and bring it outside the walls of the community in which he lives and into the world in which we live, it comes out this way: Personal prayer does not dispense us from corporate prayer. The one sustains the other.

ROBERT BENSON

When I first met Mrs. Hessie, who died at age 102, I noticed two things immediately. One was her eyes, the way they would light up, sparkle, offer greeting and welcome—more eloquent, more gracious, than any word she might ever have said. In all my years of ministry I don't think anyone I ever visited has been so visibly glad to see me.

The other thing was this: she wanted to speak, tried to speak, and did speak a little: a few slow words those first few visits—but so slowly and with such effort that sometimes she would look at me as if we were playing a game. She wanted me to finish the word, guess what she was saying, fill in the blanks, so we could move ahead in the "conversation."

In time, she was unable to speak at all—though her eyes still sparkled and her body still rocked. So I did the talking, read her the Psalms, mostly, and more than once Psalm 71, which I read when I buried my own grandmother.

I always lamented that I met her after her real talking days were behind her. I can only imagine what stories she might have told about her family, her church, her children, her roses.

I lamented, until one day, by chance or by grace, I came across a line from Isaac the Syrian, an Orthodox saint: "Speech is the organ of this present world. But silence is a [sacrament] of the world to come."[1]

"Speech is the organ of this present world." Words are the best we can do on this side of the Jordan. And words are good things, beautiful things, though they can be used for bad and ugly purposes. The human tongue was created for praise, but, to our shame, we may use it for cursing. It is by *speech*—whether songs, creeds, books, or testimonies—that, in the present world, we glorify God. Speech is the organ of this present world.

"But silence is a [sacrament] of the world to come." Mrs. Hessie, good Methodist that she was, understood about sacraments. Sacraments are "means" of grace, "delivery systems" for God's presence and love. Silence is a means of such grace: when we are silent, we make room for the Almighty One, and thereby offer a praise and a prayer beyond words, beyond even our best words to say or sing or testify.

Long before she died, Mrs. Hessie was already giving God that special place, that special praise. And now too, we believe and trust, she is there, her eyes sparkling as with the starry host of heaven, her body free, moving in time to the rhythms of eternal praise.

You think she was glad to see me? Think of how she looked when at last she saw Jesus.

The Languages of Prayer

When it comes to speech, the organ of this present world, and to prayer, the means by which we open ourselves to God, we find five distinct kinds of prayerful speech—actually only four, as the deepest, highest, most perfect form of prayer is **adoration, or contemplation.** The heart of adoration is love of God for God's sake. It is the most selfless of prayers, the most silent of prayers: the pray-er revels in the presence and person of God as much as is humanly possible. And there is scant testimony to the experience, for "[those] who pray, really pray, do not talk about it much."[2]

The experience of adoration, to quote the old hymn by Charles Wesley, is to be "lost in wonder, love, and praise."[3] Wesley pictures such wonder and praise as a heavenly reality, reserved for the saved and the time to come. But a hymn by Helen Lemmel describes adoration on this side of the river: "Turn your eyes upon Jesus, look full in his wonderful face, / and the things of earth will grow strangely dim, / in the light of his glory and grace."[4]

The gift of adoration is rare, or so the spiritual masters say. God grants such moments only to some and even then sparingly. The divine restraint, say the masters, is on account of mercy: that the sacrifice of self offered on the altar of adoration, the pain upon one's "return" is too severe for most.

All prayer may by grace "descend" into contemplation. That is to say, what begins as a "prayer of the lips" or a "prayer of the intellect" may prove gateway into pure heart-praying, where prayer is a *state* rather than a word or thought.[5] But such an experience, though selfless, is also intensely private.

The other four types of prayer are suited not only to individual praying but to corporate prayer as well. **Thanksgiving, or praise,** is akin to adoration, but has as its root some action of God, some provision or guidance or rescue, some blessing. The proper posture of thanksgiving is humility, though any blessing when mishandled may lead to pride. Also, much of our praise has a very narrow focus: what God has done for "me or mine."

I always think of Mary and Elizabeth before her when the news of the baby came; the prayers that they prayed after the news had almost nothing to do with the babies at all, but with God's great redemption: their thanks were on behalf of the poor nation and the world, not just their own new circumstances.

Confession acknowledges sin, individual and collective. "We confess that we have not loved you with our whole heart," as our eucharistic liturgy says. "We have failed to be an obedient church. We have not done your will, we have broken your law, we have rebelled against your love, we have not loved our neighbors, and we have not heard the cry of the needy." [6] Where any of those general confessions land in individual hearts, God alone knows. But where corporate pleading gives way to private, there is a danger that our motive turns from selfless to selfish.

Our elders in the faith speak of the difference between perfect and imperfect contrition. Imperfect contrition is based in fear, in the inescapable condition of being caught, discovered, exposed. The abrupt confessions birthed by imperfect contrition are aimed at amelioration: throwing one's self on the court in hopes of a lighter sentence or probation: I promise I'll never do it again. Such confessions are selfish to the core.

Perfect contrition, by contrast, is selfless: it is the awareness that an action has hurt another, has breached trust and relationship. Rather than fear of what might happen to "me," perfect contrition is concerned about the damage done to another or the Other. Confessions here are selfless, aimed at the wounded place, in hopes of restoring faith and trust, of renewing and restoring intimacy.

Excursus: The Lost Language of Confession

The church is where I can confess and be heard and find absolution—but I fear that the church has lost the language of shared confession: that we are sinners, that we all have fallen short of both the glory of God and our own expectations.

We have lost the language of lamentation too—not just sorrow for our own sins but the language of shared disappointment: that God seems so distant and silent when we need a word, that God seems removed when we need divine presence, that God seems so asleep when we need help: "Teacher, do you not care that we are perishing?" (Mark 4:38).

This language of confession—our deep disappointment in ourselves—and the language of lamentation—our deep disappointment in God: these holy prayers, these sacred conversations, born of deeply shared experience and mutual if halting faith and hope; these are precisely what Jesus teaches when he teaches us to pray. And these are precisely the kinds of prayers we seem no longer able to pray: we have lost the basic *language* of shared experience. More to the point, we have lost a sufficient *sense* of shared experience that might give rise to such a language.

Alone in the crowd. Ever *not* feel that way—even in the church? Maybe especially in the church: out of the conversation, out of the loop? It is a deep irony that connected as we seem to be, and more so all the time, what with our gizmos and gadgets and 4G networks, we can still feel so lonely—and more so all the time: more and more *dis*connected, isolated. Why is that?

The culture works to divide us, one against the other, into interest groups, factions, affiliations. . . . We have been taught well and have come to believe that we are on our own mostly; that we stand alone, that whatever we suffer or celebrate, enjoy or have to endure, we do so privately.

Maybe we stand with a few other like-minded folks, but we seem to have lost a sense of broadly shared experience, a language of deeply shared conviction, and so we are left mostly alone with only personal experience and personal preference to guide us . . . and no easy way to form or deepen the kind of substantial and abiding community, the shared experience and deep discussion Jesus seems to expect of those who follow him.

Intercession, likewise, may be more or less selfish. When our concern for others is really a concern for self—if something happens to them, what will happen to me—then the prayer for others is still self-absorbed. When the concern of the pray-ers is for the other (or others) apart from where the concerns might touch those of the pray-ers, the prayer is indeed selfless.

Petition is, by and large, as selfish as adoration is selfless. Jesus did tell us to offer petition, of course—for daily bread, for guidance away from temptation, for deliverance from evil—but those petitions are to be prayed with and among others.

When I teach, I often suggest to my students that they avoid petition altogether: that if we are praying our intercessions well, all of us get prayed for far more often and more comprehensively than we could when praying for ourselves. Of course, that might be a selfish thought too.

Jesus' Prayers

Jesus actually prays. Luke tells us that more than any other Gospel writer. All the time. The disciples saw him pray. And seeing *him* pray, they knew they did not know how to do it themselves, not as they ought. And they wanted to learn, to know how, and so they came to Jesus: "Lord, teach us to pray" (Luke 11:1).

They were starving for authentic prayer—as perhaps we all are. But when people are starving, you do not overfeed them. Too much food at once to starving people will kill them. And so Jesus gives the disciples tastes. Nibbles. Sips. Enough to sustain but also to whet the appetite: Jesus says,

> *When you [y'all] pray, say:*
> *"Father, hallowed be your name,*
> *your kingdom come.*
> *Give us each day our daily bread.*
> *Forgive us our sins,*
>   *for we also forgive everyone who sins against us.*
> *And lead us not into temptation."* (Luke 11:2-4, NIV)

The prayer Jesus teaches them is not everything they will ever pray, and even this same basic form of the prayer will be embellished with time and usage; but we have here the daily minimum requirement of all three spiritual food groups: intimacy, distance, and dependence.

Intimacy: Father. Jesus teaches intimacy with God, which is something we are wired to want but programmed to avoid. That is, God has made us to desire what only God can give—the divine self—and we will remain unfulfilled, unsatisfied until our deepest desires are gathered up in the Father's presence. We have been taught to avoid intimacy, to imagine that we are sufficient unto ourselves, to fear that we are in this alone. . . . But Jesus is reprogramming us for intimacy.

And *distance*: Hallowed be your name. Jesus teaches distance from God too. God is Father, but God is also spirit, while we are dust. God's ways are not our ways; God's thoughts are not our thoughts (Isa. 55:8). God is to be reverenced, approached humbly—confidently too, yes, because God is our Father—but humbly because God is the heavenly Father. "Holy Father," would be another way to render it as Jesus teaches: God is approached neither too familiarly nor too fearfully.

Dependence: There are three separate petitions in this prayer: Give! Forgive! Protect! All of them voice our dependence.

Holy Father, give. Bread for the day. And for tomorrow. Not too much—because we do not do so well with excess—but enough. Asking God to give is a confession that we cannot provide for ourselves, a confession of how dependent we are. I suspect that if the economic meltdown has given us no other good gift, it has given us the hard lesson that when it comes right down to it, all of us are radically dependent creatures. What we need most—whether food or work or healing or a sense of meaning, a word of hope or salvation: those things are grace, come to us by grace, are nothing other than grace. God's good gift. Holy Father, give.

Holy Father, *forgive*. How many things have we done that we should not have done? How many things have we not done that we should have? Lots of them, all of us. And it is not just that we do and do not, but that we are and are not. However, if we cannot speak the deep truth of our condition, if we do not confess to God and one another, do not ask for forgiveness, we cannot hear the promised word of forgiveness. Having lost the language of confession and forgiveness, we languish in a kind of guilt and regret that leaves us suffering, alone.

Is anyone afraid that people will know a deeper truth about us than we are inclined to share? Anyone more afraid they won't, so that we remain *un*known, strangers indeed?

What stands between us and you, Holy Father, remove it. And we will work to remove the things that stand between ourselves and one another. That is hard work, removing the barriers that stand between us; but that is the work to which we are pledged as members of Jesus' family.

Holy Father, *protect*. We are weak. You are strong. We are unequal to so much that faces us . . . and should the devil decide to sift us like wheat, how shall we survive? But you are able to protect us.

Now, that's a prayer, y'all. Father: Holy Father: Give. Forgive. Protect. Amen.

There are other prayers to pray, but these are a good first course for those who find themselves spiritually hungry, a primer for people just learning or learning again to pray.

And there is this: Jesus teaches us to pray in the first person plural. The first person plural is a *pastoral* form of praying, a formational prayer: we, as the children of God, praying with and for one another. The first person plural is a *prophetic* form of praying, a transformational exercise, as the corporate nature of our prayers stands in sharp contrast to the atomized and fragmented culture. Prayers in the first person plural are also *evangelistic*, inviting others to be a part of us and our praying.

Give us! Forgive us! Protect us!

These are prayers we pray together, prayers of dependence and interdependence. There is power in such praying—to form and transform and welcome, and when we pray these prayers together, we are on our way to fluency in the mostly lost languages of shared faith. We begin to speak the language of dependence, because what we ask of God we ask of our friends, as well: help me, y'all; forgive me; stand with me.

Speaking in those tongues, we will know that we have learned to pray as Jesus taught us.

Prayers Given and Received

Lauren Winner, in *Mudhouse Sabbath*, writes that when she approached her Bat Mitzvah, Ruby, a woman in her synagogue, took her aside and said that for all the presents she would receive in coming weeks, she, Ruby, was going to give her the most important one: a *siddur*, a prayer book. Ruby said, "A mark of being a Jew is praying to your God. This book is the way that Jews pray."[7]

Wherever such prayers are prayed they mark the prayers as Jewish. And so we think of Jonah in the belly of the whale. A most unpromising place to pray, or is it? Perhaps like the wet wilderness; Jonah, in the dark entrails of his disobedience and God's merciful judgment, the bloody remnants of what used to be alive, putrefying around him, all but burying him, and what does he do? He prays, of course. But not as we might expect: he does not pray frantic pinball prayers, but the prayers of his tradition, the words given to him by his heritage. In Jonah 2:3-10, the prayers offered are a "pastiche of verses taken from the Psalms."[8]

These words, anyplace. Any place, a place of prayer. Any gathering, a cell in the body.

I know nothing of Bat Mitzvah or Bar Mitzvah, but I quiver in the face of our Christian counterpart: confirmation. I am not equal to the task. Lord, how I know it. Still, I do my best, over the course of a few months, to teach the church's confirmands the basic tenets of Christian history, the broadest strokes of our United Methodist story and polity and the rudimentary vocabulary of our faith.

Eyes glaze. Jaws slacken. A confirmand's parent—who takes more notes than her daughter—nods off during the Aldersgate story and all the kids giggle.

What am I doing here?

I sign the group up for the Confirmation Retreat. Enthusiastic youth workers lead it, earnest Christian education professionals and a loud band too, which tries to get the kids to sing and jump and shout to the Lord. The parents and mentors sing and jump and shout to the Lord, hoping to inspire the kids; but the kids stand still, paw at the ground, cut their embarrassed eyes back and forth at one another. The scene is absurd and hilarious.

If I know anything about adolescents and adolescence, I know only this: the one daunting everyday task—and it takes herculean strength to accomplish it, if a person ever does—is to *avoid* embarrassment. At all costs, avoid embarrassment. I remember when my son told his mother, when she was about to drop him off at school, not to do anything, a-n-y-t-h-i-n-g, that would embarrass him. "Like what?" she asked. "Like *speaking*," he replied. He was in the seventh grade. Another morning he asked her to drop him off a block away so that he would not be seen in her car.

But at these events we expect kids to sing and jump and shout to the Lord. Instead, only the parents and mentors, who are past caring about embarrassment, do, which embarrasses the kids even more.

What are we doing here?

I listened to the loud music and their tastefully tattooed and oh-so-sincere lead singer. I listened to the youngish and funny speaker, him and his heart for evangelism. I noticed all the personal, private, "Jesus wants a relationship with you" preaching and the "give him praise and glory" praying, and I was amazed at how abstract so many of the weekend words sounded, even when sung rhythmically and loudly; and how abstruse the "invitation" was, even when offered sincerely; how hard all of it was to understand, even to me, and I have been at this for a while.

What is the purpose of all this?

Somewhere over the course of the weekend, I remembered the woman at the well (John 4:1-42). Jesus has gone into Samaria and sits at the well of Jacob. A woman approaches, at noon. Jesus speaks to her, which is scandalous enough, him a man and her a woman; him a Jew and her a Samaritan; him a rabbi and her a sinful Samaritan woman. He asks her for a drink. Then he offers her "living water," though she thinks he means "running water," and she says, "Sir, how are you going to get running water? The well is deep and you have nothing with which to draw."

Whatever that scene and conversation might mean, I realized that the purpose of confirmation, what we were doing at the retreat and week-by-week in class—what I am doing even when I am not sure I do it at all well—is giving these kids *buckets*.

The well of our faith is deep too, and living water everywhere beneath the surface of things, the aquifer of hope and love. But with what shall we draw? How can we gather the blessing?

These words and stories and lessons and prayers we teach our kids—these are the buckets. This is the language we borrow. We use these buckets, lower these borrowed words into the never-stagnant streams of God's graceful way with the world, into the sometimes algaed history of our faith but near the hot springs of our tradition, and we draw out meaning: life and faith and hope and love.

We can never reach the depths, our ropes being what they are, but if we do not draw out all the blessing—not nearly so—all we draw out is yet blessing. No bucket is big enough: we must draw together, and even then we cannot draw enough. Maddeningly, it would also seem that when we are most careful with our buckets, the more the water sloshes out. Bringing the buckets too near, being too careful, there is less to quench our thirst. But we draw again and draw again and hope for more.

The language of our faith—the vocabulary of Zion—is given to us. The language of our prayers too: the Psalms, preeminently; words given to us by God to speak back to God: this is the way we pray, and praying this way makes us who we are. The Psalms are our first, best buckets, bequeathed to us with directions to the wells.

But many of our wells have been stopped up, clogged and filled by the narcissisms of our culture. We are thirsting to death, left to the shallows. And like Gideon's men we are able to scoop only a little water with our hands or, putting our heads down, lap a bit at the pools.

But what if we unstop the wells? Dig again through the rocky surface of things so that together we can lower our buckets into the deeper and more refreshing waters? What if we make use of the Psalms and other prayers from the tradition to learn how to pray, and what to pray about?

Any language we can muster on our own, any language of piety, of faith and hope and love, is so limited. There are holes in our buckets. Even our "big words" are of no real help (writers say that the "big" words carry the smallest significance). We have no other or better buckets than those given to us.

Till we dive into the Water at last, let it take us completely, these little buckets are all we have. A borrowed language, to be sure, but what other language do we have? And like that day with the loaves and the fishes, when the boy shared what he had and Jesus blessed it and all were fed, these words and prayers have been given to us with Jesus' blessing and are more than enough to refresh us in the wilderness. When we sit down together, stand together, kneel together, and pray together, we are finally satisfied.

Bread and fish, vocabulary and prayers: these are our gifts. A borrowed language. But what other language is there? None—except, perhaps, silence.

Creedal Confession and Confusion

I believe in God, the Father Almighty, maker of heaven and earth. I believe in Jesus Christ, his only Son, our Lord. I believe in the Holy Spirit.

I believe I love the Apostles' Creed.

I came late to the Creeds, Apostles' and Nicene. I grew up in a church and part of a tradition where we did not do creeds. We eschewed all things memorized and most things written (save the Bible)—pastors could get themselves fired if they dared offer a scripted prayer (I know, because I was nearly one of them; long story).

We were suspicious of rote, of "just repeating" prayers or doctrines—because that was *religion*, not true faith. And if, as our preachers thundered, there were many "so-called churches that propagated religion," we all had unmediated faith in Christ alone!

That faith, if it were *real* faith, expressed itself personally, spontaneously: a matter of the heart and spirit, not memory or the page.

And so, while we learned the Lord's Prayer in Sunday school, we never, so far as I remember, repeated it in worship—for fear, as my dad often told me, of "just saying the words and not really meaning it, not really feeling it."

I understand that perspective. John Wesley understood that perspective too; shared it in some ways. He felt that what was wrong with the Church of England, his own church in his own day, was that most congregants just said the words, most worshipers just went through the motions—had a form of godliness, so to speak, but not the power thereof.

Wesley began the Methodist movement as a kind of "between Sundays revival." He had no intention of divorcing himself or his people from the established church; he simply gathered small groups of people for Bible study; for heartfelt prayer, sharing, confession, accountability.

Though I was Southern Baptist (and consequently taught to be wary of Methodists), Wesley's "between Sundays" piety is how I first experienced church and worship, and for long years assumed, both constructively and critically, that all church and worship should look, sound, and *feel* pretty much like that: spontaneous and personal, temporal and testimonial. In sum, no creeds, no prayer books, no tradition, no *religion*. Nothing, in other words, that anyone else had composed.

Except, of course, *hymns*.

We Baptists were a singing people, I mean. But somehow it never dawned on us—at least let me say it never dawned on me—that by singing hymns we contradicted our stance, experientially disproved our prejudice against things "composed."

Those old words, written by people we never knew—which is to say, they did not spring from our minds or pens—somehow in singing them *became* our words: went from the page, in through the eyes, down into the heart, and by the time they came back out again in song, they had turned into personal praise.

Words, lyrics, poetic language—*given* to us from the outside: those old words became our best, most personal, most spontaneous testimony.

Like many before me and since, I learned my faith first and best by singing those old songs. And sometimes, tears would come—and still do—because those given words landed so deeply, helped me say truly and eloquently from the heart what I most likely could not have articulated otherwise, at least not with that depth and eloquence. Left to my own imagination and vocabulary, my personal faith and experience, I simply could not have said, sung, or trusted such "wonderful words of life," as it were.

Given languages. There are many prayer languages that are "given" languages.

I have been thinking about the various languages of our faith, delivered to us much as the faith itself is delivered to us. What prompted this new wave of thinking was a clergy-support meeting some weeks ago when my friend and colleague Tom rather quietly admitted that he is what folk used to call "charismatic." He "speaks in tongues," as does my friend John, a pastor in another denomination and state.

I have never had the experience myself. In fact, I used to be quite distrustful of "the gift," even disdainful, mimicking the malediction of one of my professors in seminary who was, as I was at the time, painfully aware of the kind of schismatic power prideful expressions of the "charismatic movement" could have in a local church. He denounced glossolalia as "baby talk."

Then I met John, a student at the same seminary—and in that same professor's Greek exegesis class—who began to teach me otherwise. I still don't understand glossolalia, have never really gotten it. But because I love and trust my friend, I can yield to a reality beyond my personal experience.

I shared my professor's (and my own) reservations about "tongues" with Tom when he hesitatingly, and rather sheepishly, mentioned his dilemma in being a "spirit-filled United Methodist." (You can make your own joke here, and there are many!).

"Most Methodists don't talk like that," he said with a chuckle. No, they don't. And in my memory a light bulb flashed. I remembered a conversation I had with a member of a church I once served, long years ago now, when I gave her a copy of John Baillie's *A Diary of Private Prayer*.

"I don't talk like that," she said.

"Of course you don't," I countered. "That is precisely the power of it. You find yourself saying familiar things in unfamiliar ways, and it opens up all sorts of new meanings."

I have long believed this to be the power of liturgy. Tom and John assure me that is the power of their ecstatic experiences.

We might say, then, that both liturgy and glossolalia are *given* languages, speech from the outside that goes in and comes out as *our* speech, if we allow it. "Yielding to the language is the key," John has said to me. "Relinquishing control."

How often I am reminded, however, that those of us practicing the liturgy of the tradition *do* try to retain control, do not yield.

For example: Sunday by Sunday we Methodists leave out a piece of the Creed: a little independent clause right in the middle, when we are talking about Jesus and how he was "born of the Virgin Mary, suffered under Pontius Pilate, was crucified, dead and buried . . ."

Right *there*, in any creedal church other than Methodist, and just before "on the third day he rose from the dead"—which is to say between Jesus' crucifixion and his resurrection—worshipers say this: "he descended into hell."

We bowdlerize the text, excise that piece. Why?

The short answer is that John Wesley himself couldn't make up his mind about it. When, in 1784, he designed the Sunday service for American Methodists, he included the phrase here and there: in the Creed, in the liturgy for baptism. But he left it out in other places (his revision of the Articles of Religion, for example).

American Methodists have been ambivalent ever since. Or maybe not so ambivalent—by 1792, only eight years after Wesley's instructions, we quit saying it. At all. Not in the Creed, not in the baptismal liturgy.

Only in the last few decades, with the impetus of the ecumenical movement, as we have tried with others to reach back past our differences, to find common ground in the more ancient articulations and practices of the church, has the phrase reappeared in our hymnals and worship books, and then, often, just as a footnote.[9]

Okay. So what?

A couple of Lenten seasons ago I began the practice of saying the Creed several times each day. Slowly, pondering. And I started including "he descended into hell." I have reclaimed that language for myself, not just for fidelity to the greater tradition but for the greater comfort the *un*-bowdlerized Creed can afford, and more than the revision. For me, as I survey and examine the truth of my life—as I try to muster enough courage to do that: to look at myself honestly down there in the depths—the question for me is not "*Did* Jesus go there? To *hell*?" Which may have been Wesley's hang up.

The question for me is "Would Jesus go there?" Would Jesus be willing to go, *wherever*, even to hell if it came to that, for the sake of his suffering children, wherever they are when they need him most?

I find great comfort in the suggestion that he who in his life and ministry loved the lost, the sick, the dying—that in death he would not be done with his ministry at all but somehow work even then to seek and save those who most needed seeking and saving. That our Lord would go even into hell for his love of those who knew the hell of being out of union with God.

Removing that independent clause ("he descended into hell") removes a deep truth and a deep comfort too, I believe. Whenever we presume to bowdlerize a text, whether a creed, a psalm, a hymn—even in the name of "inclusion"—we might instead be performing our own act of exclusion and not just of a few words but of many souls.

In addition to the Creed, *The United Methodist Hymnal* savages many of the psalms, truncates whole sections that do not seem to "fit" one way or the other with our current sensibilities. We claim that uncomfortable verses (Ps. 107:17-22, for example) say things about God we do not believe. And yes, Wesley himself said that some of the words of some of the (imprecatory) psalms are not fit for Christian lips. Still, our excisions may say more about *ourselves* than we imagine. I believe we are also removing a big chunk of the promised comfort from those who have experienced or are experiencing exactly such a thing as the psalm describes, who might hope for a time when they, as *the redeemed*, might say so.

We might let Linus be our guide in these matters, whose sister, standing at the window and looking out on a day so rainy she thought it might be the end of the world, found comfort in his story of the rainbow. "Sound theology" has such power, he says.

The doctrines, the prayers, the promises: when the words are on our lips and tongues we can taste and see that the Lord is good (see Ps. 34:8). Standing at our own windows, in the middle of our own wildernesses, fearing what we fear, we can say the Creed, sing the

THE LANGUAGES of PRAYER

songs, pray the prayers, feel the Spirit—and see, know, trust that we are not alone to face whatever it is we are facing.

The Creed, to me, is a hymn that teaches me my faith week by week as surely as the hymnals of my childhood. It is a song of praise, a reminder of God's promise. Written so long before I was born, it is as fresh and new as right now, with the power to bear me up in troubled times.

And tears sometimes come to say it . . . to remember that by means of this "sound theology" believers have endured whatever they have had to endure, have gotten through it, whatever it was they faced, faced even death and died at peace—with these very words on their lips.

Such is the power of our theology's sounds, the words of the tradition, the words of the Spirit, as well as the theology found in our hymns—all the given languages of our faith.

Summary

The languages of prayer comprise both silence and speech. Voiced in prayer are adoration and thanks, intercession and confession, and petition. These five "types" of prayer, at least in their more selfless forms, do not come naturally to us and, like any language, must be learned by repetition. Jesus teaches us how to pray and also where: with each other. He teaches us to pray and to pray together, and we must learn both things at once to counter our selfish inclinations. When we learn the languages and postures of prayer, we enjoy a kind of deep intimacy that forms and reforms us as a people. In that way even our spontaneous prayers have balance, and our personal prayers are communal.

Questions for Reflection

1. Take an inventory of your personal praying: what prayers do you pray most often? Would you categorize them as "selfless" or "selfish" prayers?
2. How might you learn to practice silence or centering? What is your reaction to this statement: "Silence is a kind of sabbath"?

7

THE HOPES OF PRAYER

What we should turn away from seems clear: it is captivity to our own culture, coupled so often with blind self-righteousness. But what should we turn to? How should we live as Christian communities today faced with the "new tribalism" that is fracturing our societies, separating peoples and cultural groups, and fomenting vicious conflicts? What should be the relation of the churches to the cultures they inhabit? The answer lies, I propose, in cultivating the proper relation between distance from the culture and belonging to it.

MIROSLAV VOLF

When we gathered to honor Jack and worship God, I recalled at the graveside that by the time I became his pastor, the former truck driver was already gearing down, idling a little on account of his eyesight. When he finally turned the truck off at last, it was his wife, Frances, who did the hauling, took him here and there because it was no longer safe for him to drive.

I saw them at church, mostly, and how faithful they were to be there. I was faithful to stop and speak. Sunday by Sunday I would take Jack's hand as he offered it. He could not see me, was not able to find my hand, blind as he had gotten; he just extended his hand toward the sound of my voice. I could see his hand, of course, and so

I would take it and shake it, kind of cradle it and chat for a moment or two.

You could find worse images, I think, for our posture before God—all of us extending our hands, perhaps feebly, unable to see who or where exactly we are reaching, just offering our hands toward God's voice; but God can see us, better than we can see God, who takes our hands and draws us close, near to his heart and at the last, into his home.

Until then, "You are the light of the world," Jesus said to his disciples (Matt. 5:14), speaking to all of his disciples, then and now, them and us; and, as is almost always the case, he speaks in the second person plural. "*Y'all* are a city set on a hill, which cannot be hidden." But often we are not light. Often the "city of God" is in fact invisible.

Not the church itself, its building and structures. Rather, the buildings and structures, the management and maintenance, are often the baskets we put over the candle. Soon, starved, the flame dies.

"No one," Jesus continues incredulously, as if he can see what often becomes of us and his church, "lights a candle and puts it under a basket. Rather, the candle is placed on a stand that it might give light to the whole house. And so let your light shine," he says by way of invitation, challenge and command, that the dark and cold and frightened world might see to find its way to me and to a better way forward (Matt. 5:14, my paraphrase).

Be formed. Be transformed. Stand with one another. Stand against the fear and fragmentation. And invite others into the circle.

But with the invitation and the call and the challenge comes a crisis. Can we do this thing? Pray together? Become a people? Live as we pray? *Otherwise?*

Bad News on the Doorstep

In October, November, and December of 1999, at three successive ministers' meetings, my supervisor warned us to stockpile food, equip a shelter, get ourselves *ready*, because he was sure all the dire predictions were correct: the world's computers were going to shut down at the stroke of midnight on December 31 and throw us, quite literally, into a new Dark Age.

These days, does anyone even *remember* Y2K?

I do remember the more recent warnings and fears, some of them associated with the Large Hadron Super Collider and the plan to accelerate beams of protons to 99.999999 percent the speed of light—which led some scientists to speculate that if that happened, a black hole would form and devour the earth, and some preachers took up their sandwich boards to proclaim the end was near.

Who doesn't remember the man who said Jesus was going to come back in May of 2011 to rescue the true church from the forces of evil and also to inaugurate the world's last destructive cycle—and the Bible *guaranteed it*, he said, unaware, apparently, that the "Rapture," as people call it, is not a *Bible* concept at all. He is not the only one who has built a ministry on that false foundation, nor the only preacher to leave sad and disaffected followers in his wake (many of them now impoverished after giving up savings and land and jobs to spread the false message). People use lots of bandwidth and spend vast fortunes in hopes of getting others "Rapture-ready." It has long been so.

For hundreds of years, such preachers and predictive prophecies have left people bankrupt, homeless, waiting in fields, and, at the very least, humiliated. The entire church shares in the embarrassment.[1] Nor is the silliness limited to Christians. Recall the recent Mayan calendar thing.[2]

So what is it about us humans and our fascination with "the end of the world"? There are so many end-of-the-world scenarios, some of them writ large and some of them more localized. Some are barely a blip on the radar, but others prompt vigils and mass suicides and all sorts of craziness. Remember Hale-Bopp?

So why are we humans so susceptible to this stuff?

The question is not original with me. I first saw it proposed by Miroslav Volf, a Croatian Christian theologian who teaches at Yale. Why, he wondered on his Facebook wall, are we so fascinated by, enamored with, and vulnerable to the fear of ultimate judgment and destruction?

He answered his own question this way: because somewhere deep down, most of us believe the world is so broken as it is, so *not* what it is supposed to be, so irretrievably and unsalvageably corrupted, that it deserves to end, needs to end. And no matter whether Jesus comes back or the calendars run out, time needs to stop—or start over.

Maybe another flood! A massive tsunami, a great cosmic bath, to cleanse the face of the earth, to wash it all away! Only that did not work last time.

Or a great conflagration! The earth dissolving in fire or purged of its evil—by a nuclear holocaust, a catastrophic volcanic eruption, or an asteroid strike!

Perhaps all of us, now and then, are ready to don the sandwich board and proclaim that the end is near, if only because we have the deep sense that "it can't go on this way." Only, it *does* in fact keep going on in just this same way, only more so. Add fear and panic—whether of gunmen, politicians, terrorists, or foreign powers—fold in social media and sensationalist commentary, stir with bad hermeneutics and cryptic documents, calendars, and such, and the fragmentation deepens.

So much of the bitterness and animosity that characterize our nation and our world, the war and violence and enmity that break us apart, that make us wish, sometimes, for the end of the world or sometimes fear the end of the world—though we could almost concur if it came—all of that fragmentation, that anger and division, depends on an "us-them" mentality. It comes from a more or less narrow tribalism: us vs. them: Jew vs. Arab, American vs. Soviet, American vs. Russian or Chinese or whatever, Republican vs. Democrat, Christian vs. Islam, faithful vs. pagan. There is "we" and there are "the others," and whoever the others are, we are sure that they are the problem, whatever the problem is. And whoever "we" are, we are sure that we are right, that we are righteous, that we are God's people with special place and privilege. . . . We/they, us/them, and never the twain shall meet.

That kind of divisiveness, anger, brokenness, those fragmentations and estrangements, proves and fully demonstrates our sin. And when shall God end such fragmentation, heal the brokenness in our world, our country, our relationships, our own hearts? And by what means shall that healing come?

The Table, of course—for Christ invites to his Table all who love him; who repent of their own sin and seek to live in peace with one another.

And the Font too—where we are initiated into Christ's holy church, incorporated into God's mighty acts of salvation, and given new birth by water and the Spirit into the people and purpose of God.

We pray prayers at the Table and the Font: the Great Thanksgiving for bread and wine, the Thanksgiving over the Water. These prayers bring us close and send us out. By means of the sacraments we are reconciled to God and one another, and by means of our prayers we are given the ministry and message of reconciliation. We who were far off are now near; we who were no people are God's people; we who had no purpose have this purpose: to live for the praise of Christ's glory and to invite others to be a part of the great thing God is doing: reconciling the world to the divine Self, not counting our trespasses against us but sending us into the world as agents of Christ's peace.

End of Prayer as Its Beginning: Light and Darkness

Our elders and betters in the faith use many images to describe prayer's path and fruition. One image is *illumination*: we journey from the darkness into the light—from confusion and doubt into clarity and faith. Examination, purgation, illumination.[3] That formula for prayer progression is almost intuitive and all but normative, at least in the West.

The Orthodox, however, speak of prayer as a journey not into the light but into the darkness: a descent into mystery. In the context of the church and through the lens of sacraments and scripture, we consider nature or the things of nature—a prayer referred to as *physiki*.[4] Then we may consider the source and substance of these things: God.[5] Some people will come to use images, icons, and symbols as "thin places" or vistas through which to view something of the Divine. Such praying is *kataphatic*. But then a pray-er may begin to consider God apart from nature, apart from symbols or images too; in fact, apart from any externals: *apophatic* prayer: prayer without images. To pray apophatically is to enter the "thick darkness" where God is, as Exodus 20:21 describes it.[6]

And who else might be there?

One Sunday night, when I was a very young boy, I was standing with my father and a few others—a thin remnant of the morning's only slightly larger "crowd"—in the gravel parking lot of the little Baptist church Dad was serving at the time. Most of the evening worshipers were already gone or in their cars, but the ones who were still hungry, who had not heard enough, nested around him like baby robins—and he fed them just so: regurgitating his sermon till, finally, they were filled. I stood a polite half step behind him, but at his back—I was his biggest fan and his rear guard. I loved that place, and I loved that time. I loved Sunday night worship, when we sang all the heaven hymns, a reminder that God was great and God was good and even though we had sinned and fallen short, God loved us anyway. I loved hearing Dad preach, even when it was about sin, as it was that Sunday night: Adam and Eve and the Garden and the snake and the fruit and the wages of sin. But the gift of God, the gift of God is eternal life. I knew that *especially* on Sunday nights.

Later, I would come to learn that "evening" was the beginning of a new biblical day: that Jewish time begins at night, in the darkness, when there are few lights. God's time is the evening, and God's place is the darkness: into the darkness God comes and into the darkness God speaks; and out of the darkness God creates all God creates, using whatever might be found there in the broiling void and chaos. God waded into the darkness much like Jesus entered the Jordan. God created the heavens and the earth, "and there was evening and there was morning, the first day" (Gen. 1:5).

And early on another first day, after a very bad week, and while it was still very dark, God *re-created* the heavens and the earth, God's ruined Son and us too.

It came to that only because another day, long before, in the cool of the evening when God came looking for Adam, God found Adam hiding and afraid. I, a son of Adam, knew that story well, how he feared for God to see that he was naked, and the only reason he knew he was naked was because he had done the one thing God had said not to do, and now there was hell to pay for all of us. At least till Easter. At least that is the way Daddy preached it, though he preached in a way that sometimes made the good news sound more like bad news, like he really believed in sin but not so much in forgiveness.

But Adam had brought this dread consequence on himself. And on us. He was to blame and maybe Eve too, but ours was the guilt. No getting around that. God had made a good earth and given it to them. God had scooped up some of that good earth and with earth's mist and holy spit and the salty sweat of God's furrowed brow, God had made mud and a mud man: had molded it, like a Potter with clay, pressing, kneading, shaping it; leaving divine fingerprints all over it. God had breathed into the mud man the breath of life— only now there was death because Adam and Eve too had disobeyed the lone commandment God had given: not this tree, not this fruit. Whatever else you want, you'll find it; eat this and you'll lose it, every good thing I have given for your enjoyment.

God had wanted relationship, had worked to create intimacy, had come looking for fellowship. Adam chose to obey a lesser god, his own passions. And now he was a stranger not only to God but to Eve too, his complicit bride, bone of his bone and flesh of his flesh and cursed with his curse. They were estranged from God and isolated from each other, hiding in the bushes like frightened animals. And it only got worse.

Worse for them, as the consequences of their selfishness and haste would kill their son Abel and make Cain a murderer.

Worse for us too. As it was in the beginning, is now and ever shall be, and getting only worse all the time, till the world shall end if ever it does.

I knew all of that. I knew that I was as guilty as Adam. All humans were. I knew all that. Almost never quit thinking about it.

I also knew that Dad and I would be passing a Dairy Queen on the way home. Dad said maybe we could stop and get me a dip-top cone. Chocolate.

Dad's voice droned. I was thinking of ice cream. Only then, Dad turned and grabbed my shoulder. Startled, I saw that he was handing me his key to the front door of the church. He told me to go back inside and get his Bible: he thought he had left it on the pulpit.

I took the key, turned and walked the fifteen or so steps to the door, unlocked and opened it, climbed the six or eight stairs up to the sanctuary's level, then down the aisle toward the far end, where the pulpit stood. I was almost all the way there when, all at once, I realized how dark it was inside the church. It was not just dark, it was *dark*.

I stopped dead, overwhelmed.

Obedience impelled me, but fear arrested me. And what did I fear more? The darkness? Or disappointing my father? I was paralyzed.

Far behind me now, in the back wall above and to the left side of the door I had entered, there were tinted windows, almost floor to ceiling, and through them the barest glow from a streetlamp outside and down a bit from the church. But that was no light at all, not enough to rescue me. I was alone in the abyss—Jonah in the belly of the fish; Daniel in the lions' den; Lazarus in the tomb; Jesus in Gethsemane; Abram in the evening when the animals were sundered and the birds of prey came. I was terrified. Drowning in the darkness.

Whether every child is afraid of the dark I do not know. What I do know is that I have never been more terrified in all my life. My legs quit working: I could not make them go forward, on to the pulpit and get Dad's Bible; I could not make them turn me around to run out of there. I was frozen, immobilized. My heart was pounding. I could not breathe.

What if God were in the darkness? What if God had come looking for me and me guilty as Adam? For all I did not know, I was sure even then that I had sinned and fallen short of both God's glory and Dad's expectations. I was reminded of both things almost every time Dad preached—not that he ever pointed a finger at me directly, but he didn't have to. I knew my transgressions: I was born guilty, conceived in iniquity. I had eaten the forbidden fruit, even if I did not know exactly what that fruit was or how it tasted. Maybe like ice cream and chocolate, because Mom told me not ever to eat chocolate: she was sure I was allergic to it; but Daddy sometimes got me a cone on the way home from church. My sin was ever before me.

God was there in the darkness looking for me as God had looked for Adam. But unlike Adam, I had no place to hide. God could see in the darkness—the darkness is not darkness to God (Ps. 139:12)—but I could not see at all. What if God were behind me ready to put a hand on my shoulder and take me?

"If I should die before I wake," I had prayed every night since before I could remember, and maybe this was the night when I would.

How long I stood there, I have no way of knowing. Maybe only a few seconds. Or minutes. If felt like hours. Somehow, finally, I managed to quiver my way those last few steps and retrieve the Bible. I turned, and by the grace of the dim and indirect light of the streetlamp down the way I ran to the steps, jumped past them to the landing, lunged through the door. I tried to breathe, turned to lock the door behind me, then shuffled quickly back to Dad, who was still droning on as before—as if I had not gone to the edge and back, as if nothing at all had happened.

That night's terror was a half-century ago, but I have thought of it every day since, and every time I do, I remember how scared I was that God was there in the darkness, waiting for me. After long years and bitter experiences, my fears have given way to hope—hope that God in fact *is* in the darkness, waiting for me. God looks for me as I look for God, and I am not alone in the darkness. God is in the darkness even yet, looking to use whomever God finds there to make a people and a work and a world.

What fueled such hope? What turned my fear on its heels so that now I can see even the darkness as light? The Psalms. And the Jesus Prayer. And the communion of the saints. And the testimony of my elders and betters. And the Creed, the Apostles' Creed, that ancient statement of faith, words by which Christians have lived and died for centuries. It is a "summary of the faith found in the Old and New Testaments," as we say, but crafted at a time when most of the faithful could not have read a Bible even if they had one—but nobody had one. And that one line: *he descended into hell.*

He, meaning Jesus, descended into hell, to remind us that there is
no depth to which Jesus will not go to rescue his children, no darkness he will not enter, no affliction he will despise, no suffering he
will not endure for and with us. No matter our darkness and suffering, no matter the pain or estrangement, Jesus is already there with
us, to minister to us in our captivity, to bring us back to him and to
his family.

I remember that moment long ago, and its fear. But now, every
time I think of it—every time—I go on to say a prayer of thanks
to God for being in every dark place. I acknowledge that there is
no place so dark that it is not light to God—and that God is close
enough to put hand to my shoulder or breathe in my ear, that the
darkness is God's place, that the lightlessness is but the beginning of
a new day. And something better than ice cream waiting for me on
the way Home.

Light. Darkness. Both are fetching images. There are more, of
course.

Stilled Waters

The earth is so restless, unsettled, and its people too. And if we are as
unsettled as the rest of the world, as agitated and dis-eased, then what
are we more than others? How shall we, who with straight faces proclaim as if we believe it that "though heaven and earth pass away, my
word will not pass away" (Matt. 24:35; Mark 13:31; Luke 21:33)—
how shall we be *heard* if we ourselves are as terrified as the rest—if *we*
fear what *they* fear? If we spend our days as frightened as those who
have no hope, then they will have no example in us, will not see Jesus
in us, or proof of Jesus' word or Jesus' peace dwelling in us.

Think of your life as a pool of water, a pond or small lake. When
the water is still, what do you see on the surface of your life? Whatever is reflected. For Christians, what we want to reflect is Jesus, the
love of God—that is the goal, to reflect the light of the Savior, the
pure peace of Christ: to let others see Jesus reflected in us. Whatever
helps us reflect Jesus is good stuff.

Think of the church, likewise. When the church is still, at peace, but not motionless, for in healthy water there are all sorts of life and movement and energy, the church too reflects light, is transparent in places to its undersurface light.

What happens, though, is that day to day, pebbles and rocks and trash get thrown into the pool: problems, arguments, circumstances. Boulders crash the surface of the still waters: death, divorce, diagnoses; and when they do, three things immediately happen:

1. The surface of the water is troubled, agitated.
2. All the silt, the dead stuff, the mud and thick muck that was resting at the bottom of the pond—there but still—gets churned up.
3. The water no longer reflects *anything*, is too cloudy with movement and mire to receive light or give it back.

Sometimes, when we are disturbed, we tend to answer the disturbance with more agitation, with movement, with noise and activity. But that only churns up more silt, makes it harder for us to reflect peace.

During the first summer of the Great Recession, a colleague stood on the floor of our annual conference to confess his fears before God, the bishop, and everyone else that he was terrified, *terrified*, he said, that he might lose part of his retirement benefit. I have no doubt his concern was genuine, but in the room were people who had lost far more: jobs, homes. A shiver went through the room, an unspoken incredulity: Did not this man who preached the gospel believe the gospel, that though "heaven and earth [much more the Dow Jones] pass away," God's promises would not pass away (Luke 21:33)? How often had he sung, "God will take care of you"?

I was aghast. But before he sat down I found myself thinking, *It is not just preachers.* Church members and churches too—all of us—are so afraid. Afraid of sacrifice, of loss, of change, of the future, of the past.

Fear: that is the poisoned fruit offered us day after day as we stand in what is left of the Garden. Subtle and not-so-subtle serpents on the radio and television offer us knowledge that will open our eyes to see the truth, the high-level conspiracies that are keeping us blind. We eat the fruit and find ourselves Adam-ized, fearful and hiding, isolated and agitated. We blame and rebuke. Everyone is an enemy. We must arm ourselves. We must preemptively strike. We agree with only some. Trust a few. Love even fewer.

What is *prayer* then? Prayer, I think, is calming ourselves in the presence of God and putting ourselves in position to let God calm us; giving ourselves to God's giving to receive what we cannot attain; saying words that are not ours, but words that may become ours in the saying of them, so that all our silt settles, so that our lives can catch the light of Jesus again and let it shine forth again. We pray prayers given and received, say words both familiar and unfamiliar, stand shoulder to shoulder and kneel side by side, day to day with our spiritual friends, another link in the unbroken chain of God's unending praise.

True prayer, settling prayer, giving our self and our agitation over to God's tranquility takes time and stillness and silence: waiting, listening, receiving. It takes community, others who teach us by their presence and variety that God loves all, not just many or a few. And prayer's fruition is this: we are formed as a people, marshaled to stand against the islandated disquiet of the day, and invited to invite others into Christ's peace. That kind of praying is hard work and that is why we need help. The help of one another. The help of our elders and betters in the faith. And the help of God.

Give Us the Gas: A Parable

On Easter evening the disciples are locked away in the upper room, the doors and windows closed and bolted. They are in a deep darkness, both literal and figurative, and unaware that the New Day has already begun.

They are huddled away *together*, if you look at it one way, for fear of the religious and military authorities. But they are isolated too; each of them in his own way, siloed in his own heart and mind by guilt, regret, shame, and fear.

But Jesus came in anyway: into the room and into each heart, and he gave them his peace.

And how did he do that?

Think of the spy movies you have seen. Inevitably there is a scene when the secret agents are on the run, holed up in a room somewhere, and they close and lock the door and maybe put some furniture in front of it too. But no matter how well they seal themselves in or barricade the door, no matter how tightly they lock the windows, soon wisps of smoke, gas, begin to seep in: under the door, through the transom, out the ceiling ducts. They cover their faces but to no avail. Soon they awaken and one way or the other get on with their mission.

You could find weaker images, not only for Easter evening but, later, the coming of the Holy Spirit upon the disciples at Pentecost. I think of us, so *defended* in so many ways, so isolated and alone, even when we are together. We close all our doors and windows, move our stuff around to protect ourselves from strangers. We have eaten the poisoned fruit, and now our eyes are open to see that "alone" (more or less) is safer than "relationship" or wide hospitality, because there are bad guys in the world and even in the church, bad stuff can happen if we let strangers in or too close. Don't the serpents tell us that you can't trust, you can't talk, you surely can't confess or let down your guard? And so we work hard to defend the emptiness, only to find that we are also defended against the Stranger too, the Outsider who is the Christ.

That is the bad news.

This is the good news: here comes the Gas. God refuses to leave us warrened away in the fortresses we build for ourselves, will not abandon us to our own defenses or leave us isolated alone.

No, God loves us; has ordered that we be taken: brought *out*, if you look at it one way, out of our own fearful, barricaded rooms and hearts and fears and prejudices. God has ordered that we be brought *in*, if you look at it another way, into the light of day, back into life and joy and hope. God wills us to be saved from our fears, and by the power of the Resurrection *reassigned*: given new identity and new mission in the world, the ministry and message of reconciliation. We are to be the proof and the voice of God's peace and peacemaking. That is our mission, should we decide to accept it. And God will never disavow us or our work.

And so God gives us the Gas, as it were: sends the Holy Spirit in through the crevices of our hearts and lives and churches.

God sends Jesus into our barricaded places to rescue us from our isolations, to speak to us, to negotiate: come, let us reason together, says the Lord: though your fears be as scarlet, you may be whiter than snow and *fearless* (Isa. 1:18).

It is a dangerous mission for Jesus: he died once, trying to bring us out of the darkness.

It is dangerous for us too: we have been taught never to surrender; we have not been taught that what we are protecting is our own isolation and deaths.

We resist, but sooner or later we will collapse: the air is already full of God's Spirit, and we cannot stop breathing, taking in the Gas.

When we wake up, we may find ourselves surrounded by all sorts of interesting new people, and all of them friends, people who not that long ago were themselves locked in, locked out, on the margins, in the darkness of their *own* prison cells.

New Realities

The angel of the Lord said to Philip, "'Get up and go toward the south to the road that goes down from Jerusalem to Gaza.' (This is a wilderness road.)" (Acts 8:26). The angel sent Philip to a place he might not have thought to go, on a road Philip would not normally have taken . . . on a road much like the one from Jerusalem to Jericho, where, in that story Jesus told, the man fell among thieves and was beaten and robbed and left half dead.

No guarantee that would not happen to Philip too on this wilderness road, but the angel told him to go there. And he did! Good for Philip!

As Philip went down this road he saw an Ethiopian eunuch, the treasurer to the queen of the Ethiopians. The eunuch had gone to

Jerusalem to worship, would have worshiped at the Temple, but—
and the text does not tell us this, but we can know this for a fact—he
was not able to worship in Jerusalem. At least not in the Temple
precincts. If he worshiped at all, it was from a distance. Why?

He was a foreigner. Worse, he worked for a foreign government.
That he was an Ethiopian means he was not only a foreigner but also
of a different ethnicity. He may have been rich and educated—he
had both chariot and scroll—but his ethnicity trumped all of that.

And he was a eunuch too. Five times Luke calls him a eunuch, as
if Luke wants to be sure we do not miss the point. At issue is not only
this man's country and race and work but also his sexuality.

The law clearly stated that a man who, whether by accident or
intent, was castrated—which is to say, was not a man in the way we
understand manhood—could not go into the Temple (Deut. 23:1).
That was why there were Temple police at every entrance: to screen
people as they entered. How humiliating, such a body search, and
especially for a foreign dignitary. So many barriers to keep people
like him out.

Only, the Spirit said to Philip, "Go over to this chariot and *join* it"
(emphasis added). And when Philip did he heard the eunuch reading the prophet Isaiah: "Like a sheep he was led to the slaughter, and
like a lamb silent before its shearer, so he does not open his mouth"
(Acts 8:29-32). That is almost uncomfortable for us to consider: a
eunuch, reading about one who has been shorn. Also uncomfortable this truth, penned for the Suffering Servant but describing the
eunuch as well: "In his humiliation justice was denied him" (v. 33).

The eunuch too was humiliated, and justice was denied him: he
wanted to worship God but found he was excluded—by the law.

"Do you understand what you are reading?" Philip asked him
(v. 30).

"Who is the prophet talking about?" the eunuch asked Philip.
"Himself? Another? Is he talking about me?"

"The prophet is talking about Jesus," Philip said. "He too was
slaughtered. Cut. Shorn. Unjustly humiliated."

The eunuch heard the story of Jesus as good news: not only that
Another had experienced what he had experienced, but that the

Other's experience was breaking down humiliating barriers. That Other knew that the law kills, but the Spirit gives life, and that if the function of the law is always to exclude, the function of grace is always to include.

Perhaps the Spirit sent Philip, a Gentile Christian, down that wilderness road so that he might see in another person something of his own experience, might understand the gospel in no uncertain terms: that Christians, having started with the Spirit, may not end with the flesh.

The chariot came to some water. The eunuch asked Philip, "What is to prevent me from being baptized" (v. 36)?

That I am a foreigner? That I am Ethiopian? That I work for a foreign government? That *other* matter . . . all of those things kept me out of the Temple.

Philip said nothing in reply. He went into the water with the eunuch and baptized him. They went into the water *together.*

"Do you understand what you are reading?" That is what Philip had asked the eunuch (v. 30).

"How can I understand, unless someone guides me" (v. 31). The Bible is not always self-evident. Deuteronomy 23:1 and the eunuch's own recent experience tell him that he is excluded from God's Temple, from God's people and God's blessing. But in the very scroll the eunuch is reading, in Isaiah 56:4, God promises to eunuchs—to eunuchs!—a place *in God's Temple.* And not just a place: A monument! An everlasting place!

So is the eunuch in or is he out? Do we honor Deuteronomy or Isaiah? Which will it be? Both options are in the book. So how to make sense of it?

What the eunuch needs is what Tom Long has said we also need: not only someone who knows the *words* of scripture but also the *God* of scripture; who knows not only the jots on the page but the heart of the Author; who can read the cold ink in the warm light of God's embrace.[7]

And so it is good news to us too—to each of us, to all of us, so often locked away in fear, working so hard to barricade ourselves in our emptiness—it is good news how the Spirit keeps seeping into our closed rooms so we can breathe the liberating air of the Spirit. That Jesus, our Christ, is Savior and Lord of all the world.

⎯⎯⎯ • ⎯⎯⎯

It is in prayer that we are formed, turned from isolated believers into a family of faith.

It is prayer that marshals us, commissions and inspires us to live *otherwise*, as a fearless people who stand against the fragmenting forces of our culture.

Prayer makes us hospitable, welcoming. Those who come to the Father or who would come again, come precisely through the means of grace, the sacraments and worship of the church; and when they do, they find Jesus, us, the Spirit, and the prayers waiting for them.

The End of the World (As We Have Known It)

Very calmly—and this is no small point: in contrast to the frantic, frenzied doomsday pronouncements that are always and everywhere around us—the Bible tells us the story of the wise men, the magi, the kings, or whatever we call them, whoever they were, and no guarantee there were even three of them, except that is the number of gifts they bring: gold, frankincense, and myrrh. Whoever, whatever, whether astrologers, royals, or mystics, the real point is this: they are Gentiles, which is to say, non-Jews. These Gentiles come to see the Jewish king and bring him gifts as if he is their king too, which he is.

We can *know* that this child who is born King of the Jews, the Messiah of the chosen people, is also Savior of the world and all its peoples, because these Gentiles come. Whatever, whoever, however many there are of them, they came; are the first of many non-Jews, Gentiles, who will come to worship the child.

From the very start, the Bible tells us, this child is the bridge between peoples, that all people and nations are welcome, that there is a place with Jesus for everyone.

The birth, the Baby, beckon all people to the manger: Gentiles as well as Jews, rich as well as poor, shepherds and earthly kings together, to kneel before the Lord of males and females, rich and old, slave and free. All are ushered into the sphere of Christ's blessing, which is the kingdom of God. Remember how Paul says, "Now in Christ there is neither Jew nor Greek, neither male nor female, neither slave nor free, but all are one in Christ" (Gal. 3:28, my paraphrase).

What we see in the story of the wise men is in fact *the end of the world*, at least the end of the world as we know it. It is not the end of the world as the doomsday prophets announce it, but it is the end of the world as we most often experience it. It is the end of division: it is the beginning of God's reign for all. It is the peace that Jesus leaves us, which is not peace as the world gives but peace as God intends: all of God's people, together.

I had a Facebook conversation with Dr. Volf about his question and answer. I suggested that perhaps our fascination with "Doomsday," with the end of things, is a prayer for redemption: a hope that if there is One strong enough to end the world, that same One is strong enough to heal the world.

He "liked" my Facebook comment, as if I were onto something.

Who are the people of prayer? All who come to the Font and the Table *together*. All who believe that God has made a place for us all. All who believe that God will make a place for all people and peace for all people. All who pray for the peace that God is already making. All who see the church as the house of prayer, the house of God, where there are many rooms but only one family.

All who live by the rule of their prayers and who, praying, believe that God is already making peace, here and there, and everywhere inviting us to join the divine initiative: to make a place for all God's children.

We pray for peace that we might be peacemakers, and blessed.

Lex orandi, lex credendi. Lex ora et credenda, lex labori.[8]

Summary

Prayer is the means by which we may learn fearlessness and peacemaking and evangelism. When we calm ourselves before God, trusting God's promises of the divine presence and provision, we know peace. When we silence the agitation of our spirits, we hear God's message of reconciliation and answer the call to be agents of God's redemption in the world. When we pray together, different as we all are, we are gradually formed as disciples and reformed into one holy, apostolic, welcoming people. Our communal life beckons to others to join us until we all are gathered together at last.

Questions for Reflection

1. Miroslav Volf says, "What we should turn away from seems clear: it is captivity to our own culture, coupled so often with blind self-righteousness." Do you see ways in which, on the contrary, the church seems to turn to and embrace the blind and self-righteous culture?

2. How do the images of darkness and light help you think about the power of prayer as a pastoral, prophetic, and evangelistic witness?

NOTES

-------•-------

Preface

1. Frederick Buechner, *Telling Secrets: A Memoir* (San Francisco: HarperSanFrancisco, 1991), 98–100.

2. Lauren F. Winner, *Still: Notes on a Mid-Faith Crisis* (New York: HarperCollins, 2012), 163.

Introduction

Epigraph: Eugene H. Peterson, *The Contemplative Pastor: Returning to the Art of Spiritual Direction* (Grand Rapids, MI: Wm. B. Eerdmans, 1989), 8.

1. Frederick Buechner, *Wishful Thinking: A Seeker's ABC* (San Francisco: HarperOne, 1993), 85.

2. Some scholars debate whether there was a Third Great Awakening. Others would suggest we are at the beginning of a *Fourth* Great Awakening, heralded by the emergent movement.

3. See chapter 6, "The Languages of Prayer," and my conversation with Debra Maffett, as emblematic of this perspective.

4. Michael Horton cites the well-known "secularization theory" of the sociologist Max Weber, who contends that "under the conditions of modernity," which is to say, after the Enlightenment, religion is first *privatized*, its domain shrunk to the island of private subjectivity. Once privatized, any religion's claims are *relativized*: what is compelling is no longer *truth* but *your* truth. Horton concludes that "precisely because American religion has long cherished its opposition to more traditional forms of Christianity in favor of the sovereign inner experience of the individual [self-salvation], it not only *survives* but *thrives* in [our prevailing cultural] atmosphere." Horton, *Christless Christianity: The Alternative Gospel of the American Church* (Grand Rapids, MI: Baker, 2008), 50 (emphasis in the original).

5. Horton notes that Finney, who was the preeminent orator of the Great Awakening, preached a kind of "self-salvation" that, as even Finney's critics noted, "did not even seem to require God" for success. Horton, *Christless Christianity*, 46. Horton sees Joel Osteen as preaching this same kind of self-salvation.

6. Mr. Osteen begins his sermons this way: "This is *my* Bible. I am what it says I am; I have what it says I have; *I can do what it says I can do.* Today, I will be taught the Word of God. I'll boldly confess. My mind is alert; my heart is receptive; I will never be the same. I am about to receive the incorruptible, indestructible Seed of the Word of God. I'll never be the same—never, never, never. I'll never be the same. In Jesus Christ's name." (http://www.joelosteen.com/downloadables/Pages/Downloads/ThisIsMy Bible_JOM.pdf, emphasis added).

7. Horton, this is the subtitle of *Christless Christianity*.

8. See Horton's scathing indictment of Joel Osteen in *Christless Christianity*, 65–100.

9. Jonathan Haidt, *The Righteous Mind: Why Good People Are Divided by Politics and Religion* (New York: Pantheon, 2012).

10. Haidt, *The Righteous Mind* , 96.

11. Haidt, *The Righteous Mind* (emphasis in the original).

12. Haidt, *The Righteous Mind*, 96–97.

13. Haidt, *The Righteous Mind*, 110.

14. The Third General Rule reads as follows: "It is expected of all who desire to continue in these societies that they should continue to evidence their desire of salvation, Thirdly: By attending upon all the ordinances of God; such are: The public worship of God. The ministry of the Word, either read or expounded. The Supper of the Lord. Family and private prayer. Searching the Scriptures. Fasting or abstinence." See http://archives. umc.org/interior.asp?mid=1660.

1. The Premise of Prayer

Epigraph: Alexander Elchaninov, quoted in Kallistos Ware, *The Orthodox Way* (Crestwood, NY: St. Vladimir's Seminary Press, 1979), 144.

1. The Greek verb in Matthew 6:6 is *proseuche*, which is a second person singular subjunctive.

2. I am thinking both of prosperity theology and of the "I am spiritual but not religious" language that has drawn the ire of Lillian Daniel, Alan Miller, and others. See http://cnn.it/LhuDh9.

3. See Matthew 6:1, 5, 7, 8, and especially verse 9.

4. N. T. Wright, "How Can the Bible Be Authoritative?" *Vox Evangelica* 21 (1991): 7–32.

2. The Promise of Prayer

Epigraph: Abba Anthony, quoted in *The Sayings of the Desert Fathers: The Alphabetical Collection*, trans. Benedicta Ward (Kalamazoo, MI: Cistercian Publications, 1975), 2.

1. Thomas R. Steagald, *Every Disciple's Journey: Following Jesus to a God-focused Faith* (Colorado Springs: NavPress, 2007). *The Harvest Show* (April 1, 2008, http://bit.ly/1kGErRT).

2. This is Michael Horton's term. Horton, *Christless Christianity*.

3. Joel Osteen, *Your Best Life Now: 7 Steps to Living at Your Full Potential* (New York: FaithWords, 2004).

4. I have long found it odd, sad, amusing, WEIRD, that some congregations, on their signs and otherwise, and before they tell you *anything else* about themselves, who they are or what they believe, announce that they are "independent." Is there a *worse* adjective ever to apply to a church of Jesus Christ, who called us into fellowship with him and one another?!

5. Studies suggest that robes, pulpits, modesty rails, and even rows of pews are means of keeping ourselves separated from other worshipers. In certain churches of a certain era, worshipers "bought" what amounted to box seats, complete with small gates, as "their" places for worship.

6. In "How to See a Miracle," a remarkable sermon offered at the Festival of Homiletics, Craig Barnes, the president of Princeton Theological Seminary, suggests that *thanksgiving* is the heart of the story: Jesus takes what is given to him and gives thanks. Christians, therefore, are to be distinguished from others in the world not because we are happier or more successful or more missional, but because we have been shown how to give thanks for what we have been given. We are those who have been taught *not* to join the culture's litany of lament, focusing only on what we do not have or have not been given—only on our limitations—but to be thankful for what we *have* been given. Jesus shows that such thanksgiving is necessary preamble to any miracle.

7. Haidt, *The Righteous Mind*, 247. Interestingly, a recent post on CNN suggested that at Harvard, atheists and humanists are nonetheless gathering for something on the order of "church," with songs, an offering, and so on. Perhaps the children of this culture's self-directedness are still feeling the need for "spiritual" community and that which only shared belief, of whatever source, makes possible. See http://cnn.it/1dst2i7.

8. Haidt writes, "We don't really know [the consequences], because the first atheistic societies have only emerged in Europe in the last few decades. They are the least efficient societies ever known at turning resources (of which they have a lot) into offspring (of which they have few)." *Righteous Mind*, 269.

9. See Horton, *Christless Christianity*, 23: "I do not think we realize the extent of our schizophrenia: annually decrying the commercialization of Christmas by the culture while we assume a consumer-product-sales approach in our own churches every week."

10. Henri J. M. Nouwen, *Reaching Out: The Three Movements of the Spiritual Life* (New York: Doubleday, 1975), 62 (emphasis added).

11. Dean Obeidallah, "Turn Down the Instant Outrage" (CNN, http://cnn.it/1dswutb).

12. Tony Campolo and Mary Albert Darling, *The God of Intimacy and Action: Reconnecting Ancient Spiritual Practices, Evangelism, and Justice* (San Francisco: Jossey-Bass, 2007), 131–32.

3. The People of Prayer

Epigraph: Ware, *The Orthodox Way*, 144.

1. See http://bit.ly/1acZtTO.

2. Our guide explained to us later that the "rocking" motion during prayer was a way of fulfilling the command to love God "with all your strength," which is to say, with the body as well as the heart, mind, and soul.

3. Haidt, *The Righteous Mind*, 272–73 (emphasis added). We are adaptively programmed to see "faces in the clouds" because we have evolved to be alert to anything that might threaten us (292).

4. Haidt, *The Righteous Mind*, 250 (emphasis added).

5. Haidt, *The Righteous Mind*, 257 (emphasis in the original).

6. Haidt, *The Righteous Mind*, 257 (emphasis added). Haidt goes on to say that religion sometimes or often also "blinds [people] to the arbitrariness of the practice" (257).

7. Daniel Dennett, *Breaking the Spell: Religion as a Natural Phenomenon* (New York: Penguin, 2006), 56. Dennett "is referred to as one of the 'Four Horsemen of New Atheism,' along with Richard Dawkins, Christopher Hitchens and Sam Harris" (http://cnn.it/KnsYpv; Dennett's is the twenty-second picture in the gallery).

8. Haidt, *Righteous Mind*, 266–67.

9. Haidt, *Righteous Mind*, 267.

10. "The Church's One Foundation, " words by Samuel J. Stone, music by Samuel Sebastian Wesley, *The United Methodist Hymnal* (Nashville: The United Methodist Publishing House, 1989), #545.

11. See Haidt, *Righteous Mind*, 161-64, about the Loyalty/betrayal foundation of politics and its concomitant "tribal behavior." There are many other quotes in his book about nativist behaviors.

12. For the "catholic spirit," see *John Wesley's Sermons: An Anthology*, eds. Albert C. Outler and Richard P. Heitzenrater (Nashville: Abingdon, 1991),

299ff. On "what has been believed," see *John Wesley*, ed. Albert C. Outler (New York: Oxford University Press, 1964), 46, n. 10.

13. See Nouwen, *Reaching Out*, 62.

4. The Places of Prayer

Epigraph: Abba Anthony, in Ward, *The Sayings of the Desert Fathers*, 2.

1. Kathleen Norris, *Dakota: A Spiritual Geography* (Boston, MA: Houghton Mifflin, 1993).

2. Eugene H. Peterson, *Under the Unpredictable Plant: An Exploration in Vocational Holiness* (Grand Rapids, MI: Eerdmans, 1992), 97 and following.

3. Ware, *The Orthodox Way*, 158.

4. Urban T. Holmes III, *Spirituality for Ministry* (Harrisburg, PA: Morehouse, 2002), 63.

5. Stanley Hauerwas, quoted in William H. Willimon, *Pastor: The Theology and Practice of Ordained Ministry* (Nashville: Abingdon, 2002), 60.

5. The Times of Prayer

Epigraph: Phyllis Tickle, foreword to *Praying with the Church: Following Jesus Daily, Hourly, Today*, by Scot McKnight (Brewster, MA: Paraclete, 2006), ix–x.

1. Annie Dillard, *The Writing Life* (New York: HarperCollins, 1989), 75.

2. Ward, *The Sayings of the Desert Fathers*, 19.

3. Theophan the Recluse, quoted in *The Art of Prayer: An Orthodox Anthology*, compiled by Igumen Chariton of Valamo, trans. by E. Kadloubovsky and E. M. Palmer (London: Faber & Faber, Ltd., 1966), 51.

4. Dillard, *Writing Life*, 70.

5. Eugene H. Peterson, *The Jesus Way: A Conversation on the Ways That Jesus Is the Way* (Grand Rapids, MI: Wm. B. Eerdmans, 2011), 12.

6. See my *Every Disciple's Journey*.

7. The Greek word means "God-bearer," which is colloquially rendered "mother of God." The traditional assignation to Mary, Jesus indicates that all who are faithful are God-bearers in a godless world.

8. Holmes, *Spirituality for Ministry*, 88 (emphasis in the original).

6. The Languages of Prayer

Epigraph: Robert Benson, *In Constant Prayer* (Nashville: Thomas Nelson, 2006), 51.

1. Isaac the Syrian, *Ascetical Homilies*, quoted in Ware, *The Orthodox Way*, 178.

2. Emilie Griffin, quoted in Benson, *In Constant Prayer*, 50.

3. "Love Divine, All Loves Excelling, " words by Charles Wesley, music by John Zundel, *The United Methodist Hymnal* (Nashville: The United Methodist Publishing House, 1989), #384.

4. "Turn Your Eyes upon Jesus, " words and music by Helen H. Lemmel, *The United Methodist Hymnal* (Nashville: The United Methodist Publishing House, 1989), #349.

5. See Ware, *The Orthodox Way*, 165.

6. *The United Methodist Hymnal* (Nashville: The United Methodist Publishing House, 1989), 12.

7. Lauren F. Winner, *Mudhouse Sabbath: An Invitation to a Life of Spiritual Discipline* (Brewster, MA: Paraclete, 2003), 35.

8. See *The Jewish Study Bible*, TANAKH translation, ed. Adele Berlin, Marc Zvi Brettler, and Michael Fishbane (New York: Oxford University Press, 2004), notes, 1201.

9. Heather Hahn, "Did Jesus Descend into Hell or to the Dead?" (United Methodist News Service, April 22, 2011, http://bit.ly/Knvr34).

7. The Hopes of Prayer

Epigraph: Miroslav Volf, *Exclusion and Embrace: A Theological Exploration of Identity, Otherness, and Reconciliation* (Nashville: Abingdon, 1996), 37 (emphasis in the original).

1. My favorite billboard after Harold Camping's May 2011 prediction was bought by a church with this message: "That was awkward." A Google search of "unfulfilled Christian religious predictions" or "unfulfilled rapture prophecies" reveals a plethora of such failed prognostications dating back hundreds of years. Almost no tradition or denomination is without a representative—though I could not find a United Methodist succumbing to such predictive temptations!

2. I actually had some concerns about this one when, in the months before the "assumed" date, Dick Clark died.

3. Many go on to include "union" with God on the other side of illumination; though, as Bishop Ware suggests, "the full vision of the divine glory is reserved for the Age to come." Ware, *The Orthodox Way*, 141.

4. Ware, *The Orthodox Way*, 141.

5. Ware, *The Orthodox Way*, 141. See also Chapter 4, "The Life of Cells."

6. Also see Ware, *The Orthodox Way*, 170.

7. Thomas G. Long, ed., *Feasting on the Word*, Year B, vol. 2 (Louisville, KY: Westminster John Knox Press, 2008), his commentary for Easter V, B, p. 456.

8. The law of prayer is the law of belief. The laws of prayer and of belief are the law of work. Or more freely translated: The rule/way of prayer is the rule/way of faith; the rule of prayer and faith is the way of life.

ABOUT THE AUTHOR

Thomas R. (Tom) Steagald is pastor of the Hawthorne Lane United Methodist Church in Charlotte, NC. An elder in the Western North Carolina Conference of the UMC, Tom is formerly adjunct professor of preaching, worship, and evangelism at Hood Theological Seminary (AME Zion). He is widely published in journals and periodicals (*Circuit Rider, The Christian Century, Biblical Preaching*), commentaries (*Feasting on the Word, Feasting on the Gospels, The Abingdon Preaching Annual*), and books (including *Shadows, Darkness, and Dawn* from Upper Room Books). For three years he blogged weekly for www.goodpreacher.com/. He has also blogged for theolog.org. Tom plays bass in a rock-and-roll oldies band and has two grown children.